Instant Graphics

Getting Creative with Copy Machines

by Susan Edeen and Carol Flatt

Fearon Teacher Aids
a division of
David S. Lake Publishers

 Clair and Greg
John, Billy, and Laura

Editorial director: Ina Tabibian
Editor: Robin Kelly
Designers: Emily Kissin and Terry McGrath
Cover designer and illustrator: Emily Kissin
Design director: Eleanor Mennick
Production editor: Kimberly Pesavento
Manufacturing manager: Casimira S. Kostecki
Photographer: Marge Linder

Entire contents copyright © 1984 by David S. Lake Publishers, 19 Davis Drive, Belmont, California 94002. Permission is hereby granted to reproduce the materials in this book for noncommercial classroom use.

ISBN-0-8224-3821-6
Library of Congress Catalog Card Number: 84-60319
Printed in the United States of America.
1. 9 8 7 6 5 4 3

Contents

	Concept of *Instant Graphics*	iv
	Introduction	1
Chapter I	**Graphics Made Easy**	3
	Copiers and Copy Centers	4
	Artwork	6
	Type—Words and Messages	11
	Formats, Folds, and Layouts	13
	Paste-up	14
	Encapsulated Step-by-Step Procedure for Producing Instant Graphics	15
Chapter II	**Projects**	17
	Newsletters and Announcements	18
	Playbills for Student Productions	20
	Student Government Election Posters	21
	Volunteer Handbook	22
	Flyers for Fund-Raising Events	24
	Labels and Reward Stickers	25
	Self-Adhesive Name Tags	25
	Self-Adhesive Jar Labels	25
	Self-Adhesive Bookplates	26
	Self-Adhesive Reward Stickers	26
	Stationery	27
	Bookmarks	28
	Calendar	29
	Note Cards	33
	Projects for Holidays and Special Occasions	34
	Invitations	35
	Picture Postcards	36
	Menus	37
	Holiday Book	38
	Creative Language Arts Projects	39
	Classroom Newspaper	40
	Study Unit Booklets	41
	Fingerprint Stories	44
	Vocabulary Posters	45
	Poetry Posters	46
	Stand-up Cards for Report Writing	47
	Thematic Writing Paper	48
Chapter III	**Line Art and Headings**	49
	Includes borders and frames, decorative illustrations, alphabets, pictures of animals, and useful headings	

Concept of Instant Graphics

The copy machine—a well used and readily available means of reproducing information—affords great potential for creative projects. Most school districts have large copy machines available. In addition, copy centers—businesses that offer copying services exclusively—may be located in your neighborhood. The versatility and quality of these machines make possible many quick, inexpensive, easy-to-do projects that will enhance classroom learning and stimulate fund-raising projects. With such a variety of papers and materials available for copying, results can be exciting and rewarding.

***Instant Graphics** offers numerous creative ideas that educators, students, parents, and community groups can use or adapt for use. A variety of line art is provided for these projects. The process of preparing an original paste-up for copying is fairly simple and easy to do. Step-by-step instructions take the mystery out of printing and make it fun. You do not have to be a graphic artist to produce professional-looking graphics. **Instant Graphics** enables you to become an instant artist.*

Introduction

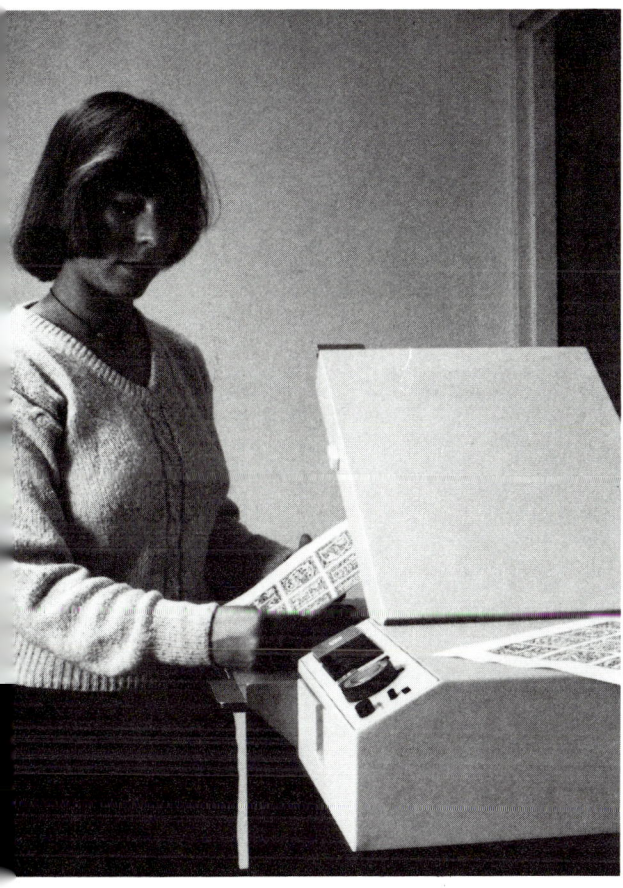

Instant Graphics illustrates how easily copiers can be used in exciting new ways. You can experiment with art, type, sizing, and color at the push of a button—for pennies. *Instant Graphics* combines the new technology of copy machines with creative, education-related activities. This book serves as a manual for amateur graphic artists, a resource for projects, and a collection of ready-to-use art for copying.

The information in Chapter I will help you to prepare any artwork for reproduction using a copy machine. First, you may need to become familiar with the kinds of copying services available to you. The versatility of copiers enables you to alter original art (by reducing, enlarging, lightening, or darkening it); collate; copy on both sides of paper; and reproduce on a variety of papers, including colored stock, self-adhesive papers and labels, letterheads, and transparencies. Chapter I also explains the step-by-step procedure for turning original art into a final, reproducible (or printable) form. Refer to this section as you prepare the projects described in Chapter II.

The activities and projects included in Chapter II have been produced by children of all ages as well as by adults. Many have been used as class projects, others as small group or individual activities. Most of the "instant graphics" applications are appropriate for student art projects. Sometimes, though, you may wish to present completed instant graphics projects (thematic writing paper or poetry posters, for example) for use in the classroom. Many projects, such as jar labels, bookplates, calendars, note cards, bookmarks, and holiday books, are suitable for fund-raising purposes.

The projects in Chapter II can be altered to fit your needs or used exactly as shown. You may wish simply to choose some other art for a particular project. Substitutions can be picked from the variety of line art provided in Chapter III of this book. The chapter is a unique collection of ready-to-use art, including borders, frames, decorative art, drawings, spot illustrations, and alphabets. They were originally drawn by artists of the past who used the fine-line drawing technique that reproduces well on copiers. This type of art (known as "clip art") has long been applied by commercial artists, designers, publishers, and advertising agencies.

You may use the designs in this book in any way you wish. Reduce, enlarge, combine, or use only portions of the art to accommodate your projects. The combination of *Instant Graphics* and an individual's imagination can open the door to original and purposeful activities for the educational environment.

Chapter I

Graphics Made Easy

Copiers and Copy Centers

Copiers and copy centers are now part of everyday life. To find a local copy center, look in the yellow pages under *Copying and Duplicating Services*. Read the ads carefully for information about the copiers and the services offered. These factors could make a difference in the projects you plan.

Most copy centers have several different machines. Copiers can reduce or enlarge and lighten or darken an image. Common reduction settings are 98%, 74%, and 65%. Common enlargement settings are 130% and 154%. When set to reproduce an image at its original size, copy machines will actually enlarge the image slightly; their 100% setting is really 102%. On some projects this difference is important. To avoid any fit problems, have your copies printed at 98% if you want your copies to be the same size as your paste-up.

Copy centers have copiers that will take 8½" x 11" standard size, 8½" x 14" legal size, and 11" x 17" paper. Several years ago copying could be done only on chemically-treated white paper. Now copies can be made on paper of any color, from heavy card-stock weight to a thin sheet of acetate (a transparency). Most machines can copy on both sides of the paper. Copiers can reproduce onto your letterhead stationery and onto self-adhesive labels. They can also copy onto transparencies of all colors. (These make excellent covers for reports.)

65% reduction

154% enlargement

Copy centers have a supply of paper in a variety of colors, textures, and weights from which to choose. Usually copy centers allow you to bring in your own paper. Check with your center to see what types of paper are acceptable for their machines. Keep your paper wrapped in its original package or in an envelope. Moisture in the paper can cause spots in your copy, so be sure to keep your paper dry.

Copy center workers are a wealth of practical information. They know the strengths and weaknesses of copiers, which copiers reproduce photos well, which copiers have just been serviced, and which ones will give you a sharp, jet-black copy. It is worth your while to learn which machines will give you the desired results. Feel free to ask questions regarding service and materials. Many copy centers also offer typesetting services, and most have a binding service as well.

Besides the speed and flexibility of copiers, one big advantage of instant graphics artwork is the low, predictable cost. You can figure out exactly what a project will cost by consulting the copy center's price list. Generally, the more copies you make, the less you pay per copy. Using special reproduction services for large quantities can be expensive, though. Experiment and plan carefully before executing final project copies. Planning ahead will help minimize project costs.

74% reduction

% reduction
(This is the same size as the original.)

130% enlargement

Artwork

Artwork adds a spark to a written message and makes people stop, look, and read on. Teachers wonder at times if *anyone* out there is reading those notes that they send home. Although there are no guarantees that artistic messages will be read, artwork *is* an attention-getting device.

The line art section of this book includes a selection of borders and frames, decorative spot illustrations, and alphabets. Feel free to cut them up and alter them in any way. Make a collage out of them. Enlarge or reduce them.

Another source of readily available art is the Dover Pictorial Archive series. This series is a collection of more than 250 books filled with ready-to-use borders, drawings, designs, and spot illustrations that have an antique appearance. The Dover series is the world's largest selection of copyright-free artwork. Your local public library or bookstore may have a selection of these books, or you can send for a catalog by writing to Dover Publishers at 180 Varick Street, New York City, NY 10014.

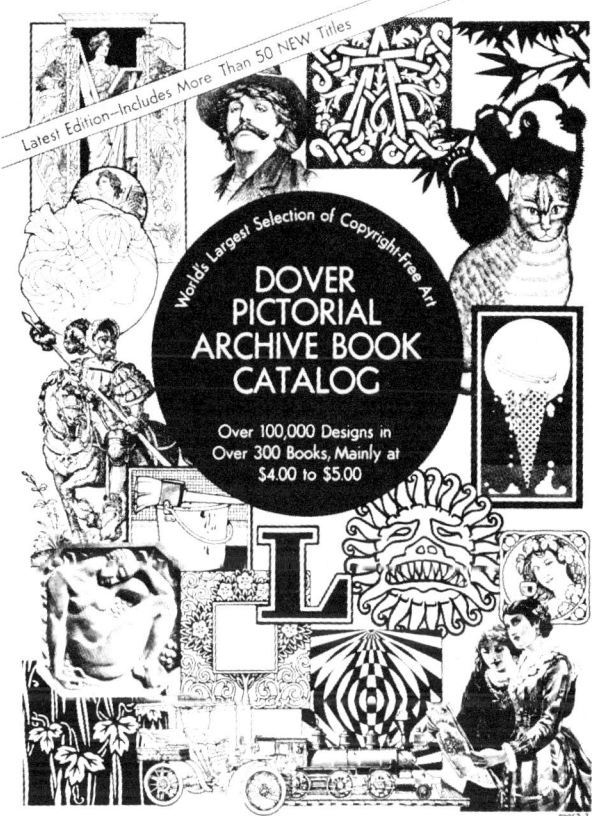

More contemporary art can be found in clip art books featuring different styles (realistic, cartoon, or decorative, for example). Clip art services have ready-made drawings from which to choose for holidays and various events. Your school's district office may have a graphic arts department that subscribes to a clip art service. You might also check with a local bookstore, art supply store, or educational supply store.

Another source of prepared art is transfer-lettering companies. In addition to producing letters, most of these companies make decorative borders and curlicues that can be transferred onto pages of written material. Catalogs are available at art supply stores.

Photographs are another fun source of reproducible art. They do not always reproduce well, though. Be sure to ask the copy center which copier best reproduces photographs.

If you would like to experiment with a "photo effect," try copying real pressed leaves, weeds, plants, or other flat objects. Collect a few leaves and plants and lay them on a sheet of white paper. Hold the leaves in place by enclosing the paper and leaves in a clear acetate folder, which can be purchased at an office supply or variety store. Reproduce the plants onto white paper. Cut them out and use the images on the paste-up.

Your best source of art is, of course, your students. Have them draw with black felt pens on white paper; good copies can be made from such drawings. If you are coordinating a class project, be sure to have the students use *fine-line* black felt markers. The points of all felt markers seem to broaden as they are used. When a group is sharing pens, the tips flatten out more and more as each child uses the pens. Starting out with fine-line markers helps reduce this problem.

Many classroom art projects lend themselves beautifully to the graphics projects described in this book. Printing techniques are particularly effective. Procedures for two printing projects—nature prints and styrofoam tray prints—are given below.

For nature prints, begin by collecting the plants that you need. Ferns or heavy leaves, such as geranium or ivy leaves, work best for printing. To make the prints, you will need a brayer, a tube of black water-soluble printing ink, and a hard, flat surface. The brayer and ink are available from art supply stores. A piece of cardboard may suffice for the hard surface, but a piece of linoleum or tile would be better.

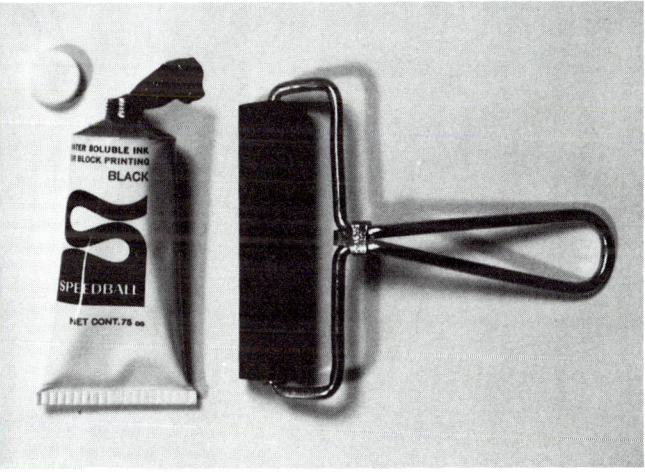

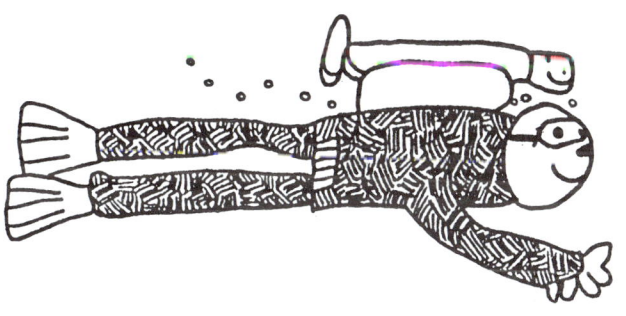

Apply the ink to the brayer and roll the brayer along the flat surface until the brayer is evenly inked. Then roll the inked brayer along the underside of each leaf. Lay the leaf, inked side down, on a piece of white paper. Cover it with another sheet of paper and gently rub your hand over it. Remove the top sheet carefully and lift the leaf from the paper. Allow the print to dry. Then cut around the leaf print to use on your paste-up.

Another printing technique that works especially well for copying is styrofoam tray printing. Styrofoam trays are usually available from meat departments of supermarkets. Have each student use a pencil to etch a design or picture on the back side of a tray. Make sure the student presses hard enough to leave definite indentations. Using a brayer and black water-soluble ink, run the inked brayer over the design. Press the inked tray onto a sheet of white paper. After the ink dries, cut around the print. A student may use the print to illustrate a poem, report, or story, or to highlight any project.

Type—Words and Messages

How to present your words and messages may seem difficult, but it is not. Your message can simply be handwritten with a black felt pen or typewritten. If you want a more professional look, you can have your message typeset at a typography shop. Your local copy center might provide this service. If it doesn't, the staff can probably direct you to a local typographer. Typographers have a large selection of styles and sizes of type from which to choose. Remember to keep it simple. Avoid ornate or flashy type styles for long messages because they become too difficult to read. Look through your favorite magazines and tear out type samples that are appealing and easy to read. Show the samples to the typographer and have your message set in a type style similar to one of your samples.

In the line art section of this book, you will find an alphabet section. Cut these up to form short headings. You will also find some fancy, narrow frames in which to write your own headings.

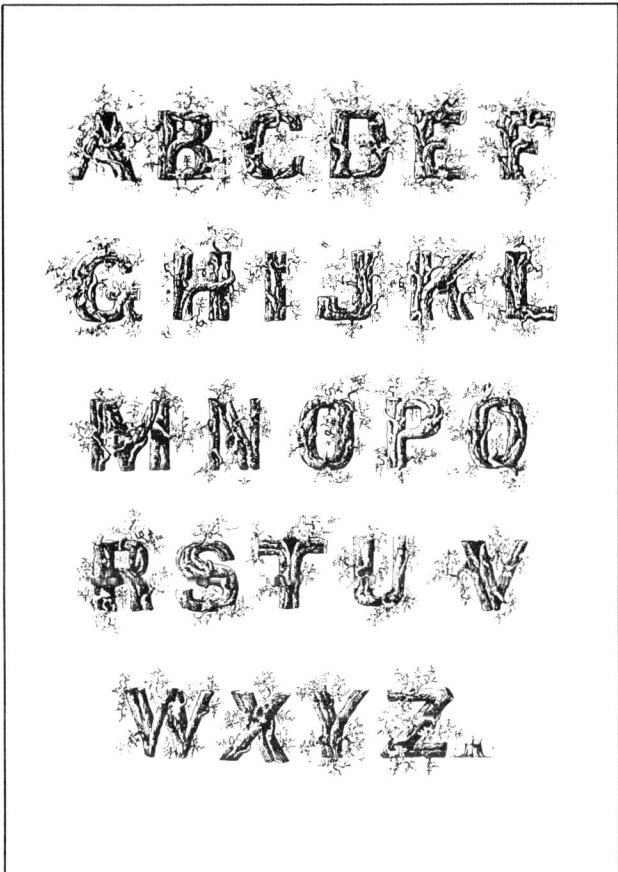

Transfer letters make professional-looking, fairly inexpensive headlines. They are sold at art stores and come in a large variety of styles and sizes. The letters and numbers are sold on sheets of clear plastic. The letters and numbers can be positioned and rubbed down directly onto your paste-up with a pencil or burnishing tool.

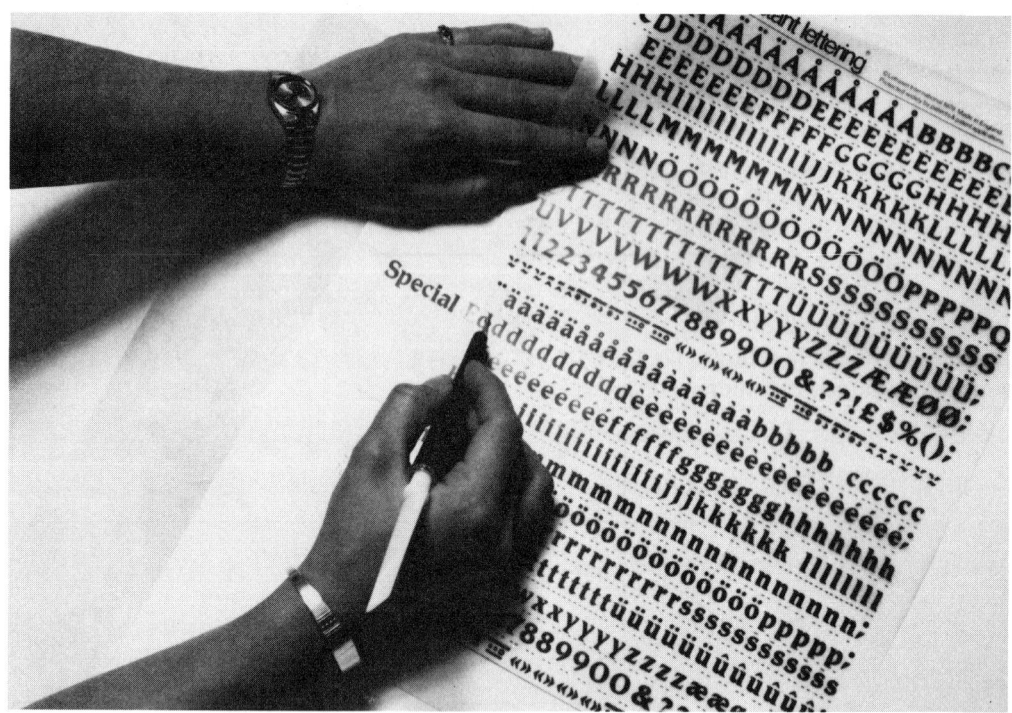

Be careful to rub down letters gently so the letters don't break. Press type to paper. You may wish to transfer letters onto a separate piece of paper and then add this to the paste-up sheet. If you need to remove a letter, scrape it off with an X-acto® blade or lift it off with tape.

Black letters copy nicely on the machines, but a more dramatic effect can be obtained by using white letters on a black background. Catalogs of transfer type with step-by-step directions for using the type are available at most art stores.

Another source of headline type can be found at stationery stores and drugstores. These are vinyl letters that you peel from a background sheet and position on your paste-up. The letters are hard to reposition, however, because of their sticky backs. The vinyl letters come in colors, but black letters make the best copies.

Formats, Folds, and Layouts

A format is the general appearance, style, and shape that your finished piece will take. Deciding on a format includes choosing the paper size and folds (if any). Copiers take 8½" x 11," 8½" x 14," and 11" x 17"

arious layouts of artwork and message

aper. Get several pieces of the appropriate paper and art experimenting with it, folding it in different ways. his will let you see all sorts of possibilities. Don't limit ur ideas to 8½" x 11" paper printed on one side. If you an to mail your copies, be sure that your folded rmat fits the envelope.

A layout is a pencil sketch on your chosen format aper indicating where your artwork and message or pe will be placed. An easy way to do a layout is to ake copies of your artwork and written message, cut em out, and arrange them on your format paper. aybe you would like the art at the top and the message low. Or maybe the message would look better on top ith the art below. Place the art in the middle with the essage around it and see how that looks. When you get arrangement of art and type that pleases you, you e ready to do your paste-up.

Paste-up

Paste-up is the final assembly of all the artwork and type in position on a piece of white paper that is the same size as your final printed product. Paste-up is always done in black and white. If you are printing on both sides of the paper, use two separate pieces of white paper for your paste-up. Paste-up materials are available at stationery or art supply stores.

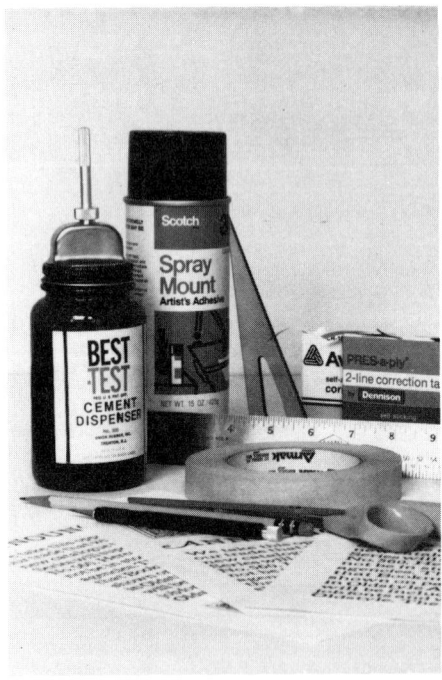  

First, reduce or enlarge your art and type if necessary to fit your format. Then begin pasting the pieces in place on your paper. Do not use white liquid glue or school paste. These adhesives will buckle your paper. One good way to paste the type and artwork down is to use rubber cement or spray glue. Use a rubber cement thinner to loosen and reposition the pieces if you make a mistake. Use a rubber cement pickup to clean the excess rubber cement from the edges of your paste-up. A word of caution: rubber cement and the pickup tool will damage transfer letters.

Another easy method is to tape the pieces down with Scotch® 3M Post-it™ Cover-up Tape. This is a lightly adhesive, white art tape. It adheres securely to paper yet removes easily without damaging the paper, and it does not show up when copied. This is the method we encourage you to use in the projects described in Chapter II.

Some of the other tools you may need are scissors, typewriter correction fluid (white), an X-acto® knife, and a nonreproducible light blue pencil. You may wish to use the blue pencil to draw guidelines on your layout. Draw lightly; sometimes copiers will pick up the blue pencil lines.

Encapsulated Step-by-Step Procedure for Producing Instant Graphics

The required materials can be found right in the classroom or in stationery or art supply stores. The materials are Scotch® 3M Post-it™ Cover-up Tape, white correction fluid, scissors, and white paper sized according to format. This is the recommended method for the projects described in Chapter II.

1. Decide on a format: size of paper, style, and places for folds (if any).
2. Sketch a layout based on the format and on the desired art and text.
3. Select your large border (or other art) from the line art section of this book. Make a good copy on white paper, reducing or enlarging it if necessary. Cut out this border and tape it in position on your layout (or another sheet of white paper). This paper is your paste-up—the original from which you will make copies.
4. Hand-letter or type the text, or have your message typeset. You may use transfer letters for large headlines. Tape the message into position on the paste-up.
5. Select any other illustrations. Copy them on white paper, reducing or enlarging them if necessary. Cut them out, position them, and tape them onto your paste-up.
6. Make a copy of your paste-up on white paper to check for any spots or shadows from cut marks. Use correction fluid to white-out any marks on the original.
7. Select the color and kind of paper you wish. If you want to see what your paste-up looks like on different colored paper, make a transparency of your paste-up by copying your paste-up onto a piece of clear acetate. Then place the transparency over paper of various colors. You can then select the final result more easily. This step is optional.
8. Reproduce the paste-up onto the paper you have chosen. Make the number of copies that you need. Be sure to request a 98% reduction because a copy machine will enlarge your paste-up slightly. On some projects, maintaining the exact size is crucial.

Step 3

Step 4
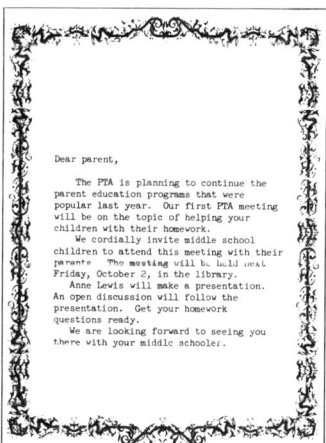

Step 5
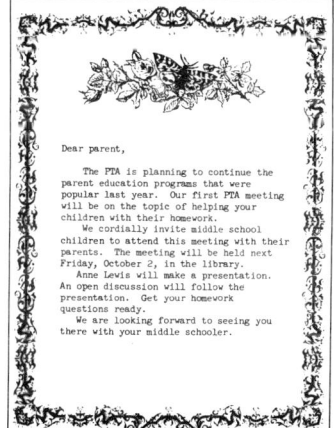

Chapter II

Projects

Newsletters and Announcements

Communication between home and school is an important part of today's education. Newsletters and announcements can easily be made imaginative and unique—and thus more noticeable. Anyone can use these simple suggestions to give notes or letters greater graphic impact.

Select a border or other line art from the back of the book. Plan your message for the newsletter and prepare your text. Copy both the line art and the message, reducing or enlarging it to fit if necessary.

On a piece of 8½" x 11" paper, paste the border and written message into position. Have your paste-up copied the appropriate number of times. If you wish to mail your newsletters or announcements, simply fold each one in half, seal or staple, and address and stamp the back side.

Paste-up of border

Folded announcement prepared for mailing

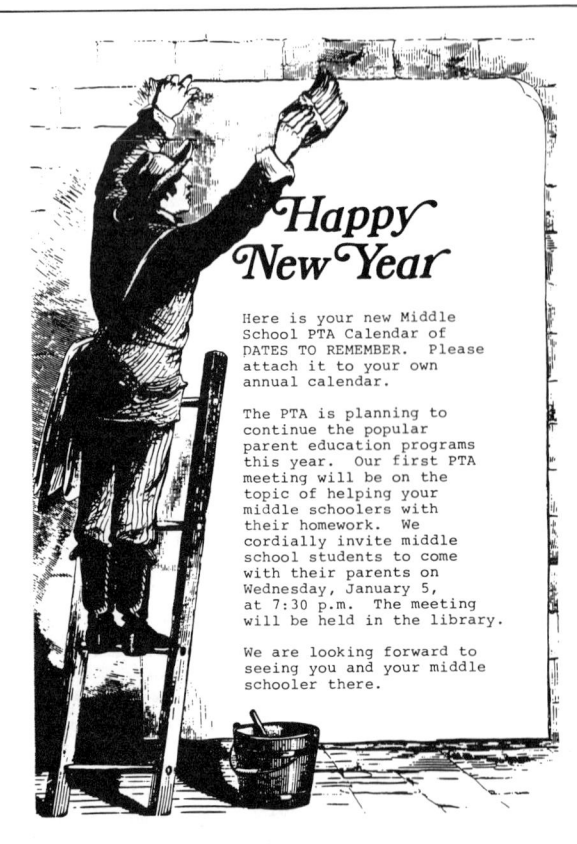

Paste-up of border and message

If the message for your newsletter or announcement is very short, you can be economical by planning a format that uses only half of an 8½″ x 11″ page. Simply make two copies of the written message and border. Paste a border and a message in position on each half of another piece of 8½″ x 11″ paper. This sheet will have two identical announcements side by side. Use this sheet as your original. Have copies made and then cut each copy in half. To mail, fold each announcement over, seal or staple, and stamp and address the back side.

Half-completed paste-up of announcement

Copy cut in half

Completed paste-up of announcement

Folded announcement prepared for mailing

Playbills for Student Productions

Plays are exciting events. All the effort and enthusiasm that go into the production should be reflected in the advertisement for the play. This project is an effective way to present the cast and inform people about the event.

Begin by acquiring student art related to the production. Place the art in a pleasing and meaningful arrangement on a sheet of 8½" x 11" paper. Paste or tape the art in place. Plan the written information to be included on the playbill. Prepare the written message and attach it to the paste-up page. Make one copy of this page. White-out any extraneous marks or shadows. Use this as your original from which to make numerous copies.

Paste-up of border

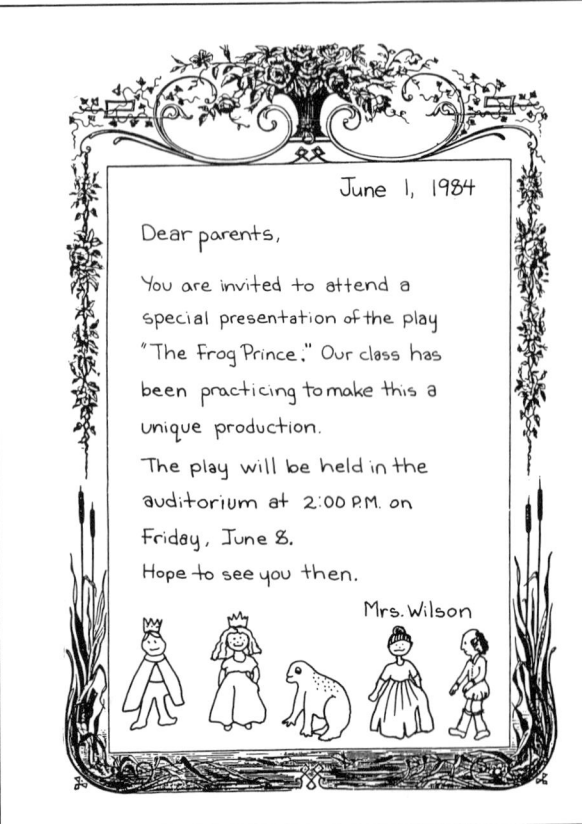

Paste-up of border and message

Student Government Election Posters

Students running for student government offices can hit the campaign trail with original, personalized posters in a variety of sizes and colors to attract the voters' attention. Posters can advertise a candidate's skills, interests, or opinions on issues, in addition to the office she or he seeks. Guide each student to the appropriate art, campaign slogans, and written messages that will advertise the individual's attributes and goals.

The student begins by selecting a photo of herself or himself. (A school photo works well.) From the back of this book, the student can choose a border suitable to the occasion. Have the picture and the border copied, enlarging or reducing the art to fit if necessary.

On a standard 8½" x 11" paper, the student pastes the border and photo in place and letters the message. If a larger poster is preferred, the paste-up can be done on 8½" x 14" paper. The poster can then be copied on paper of any color or weight. The student may wish to color in certain areas with felt markers.

Volunteer Handbook

When recruiting volunteer workers for school or community programs, provide prospective volunteers with a handbook outlining the goals and scope of the program and the duties of the participants. The handbook allows individuals to take the information home, to read it at their leisure, and to find answers to questions about the program. The handbook will continue to be useful to those who decide to volunteer.

Begin by making a "mock-up." Because the handbook project requires two-sided copying, the paste-up pages will not be in sequential order. A mock-up shows you where to place the art and messages on the paste-up sheets so that the final pages will be in the right order. Fold two 8½" x 11" pieces of paper in half and staple them together on the fold. Label the front and back covers and number the pages (the front cover is page 1). Indicate roughly where the titles, art, and messages will go. When you begin the paste-up, simply unstaple the mock-up and follow it as your guide.

You will need four standard 8½" x 11" pieces of paper to paste up this 8-page handbook. (Four sheets, not two, are needed because paste-ups are done on only one side of the paper.) Fold each piece of paper in half according to your mock-up. Begin with the front cover. Letter your titles or headings and paste them in position. The remaining space on the page is for art. If you want to use student art for the cover illustration, simply give a student a piece of paper that is the same size as the space available for the illustration. Have the child draw with a black felt marker. Paste or tape the drawing in position. If you want a title, heading, message, or art for the back cover, prepare it in the same manner.

On another piece of folded paper, type your messages for pages 2 and 7. Letter the titles or headings and paste or tape them down. If there are any illustrations, paste or tape them in place next. Continue with pages 6 and 3 and pages 4 and 5, typing the messages first, then applying the lettered titles or headings and the art. Follow your mock-up or the guide shown above.

Have the four paste-ups copied onto regular weight paper. You may wish to clip the page 1/page 8 sheet to the page 2/page 7 sheet, and the page 6/page 3 sheet to the page 4/page 5 sheet to indicate which pairs of paste-up pages will be printed back-to-back. Fold your printed copies in half, insert the inside pages, and staple them together.

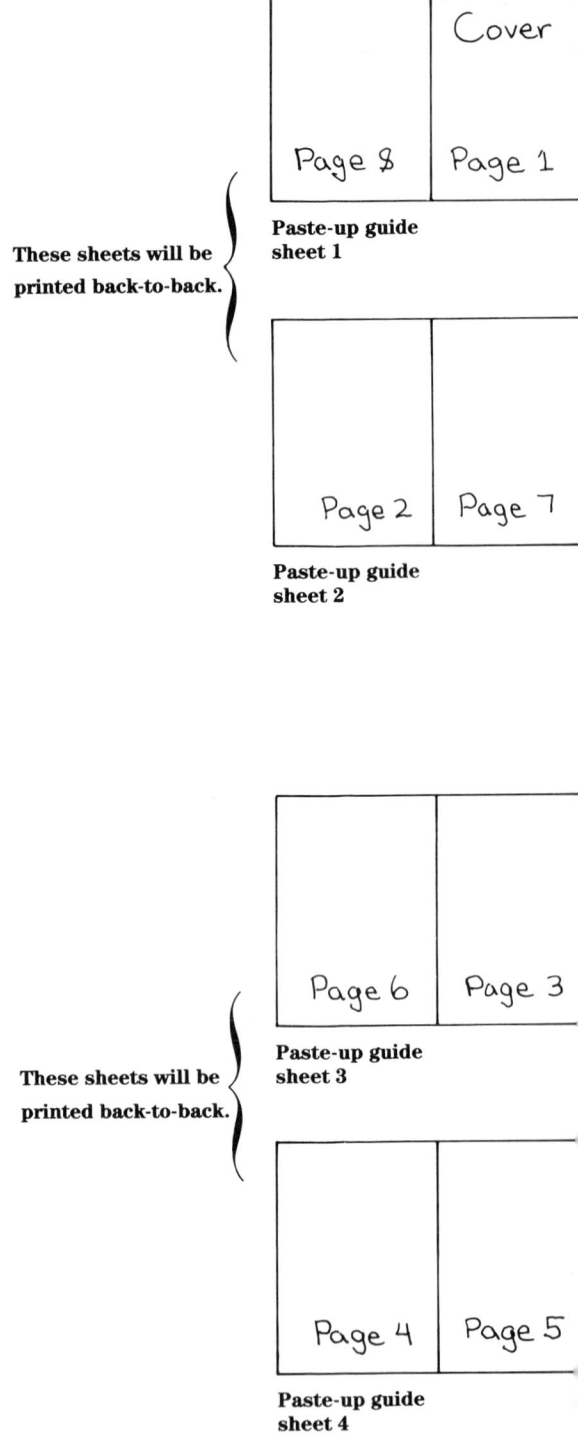

Projects 23

Paste-up procedure for pages 1, 2, 7, and 8 of handbook

Blank back cover

Completed paste-up of front cover

Volunteers are important people

Volunteers enrich education tremendously. They increase learning opportunities for all children by assisting teachers and other school personnel. Volunteers provide more individual help for all students by lowering the adult-student ratio. They provide a richer educational program by adding their own unique skills, talents, understanding, and time. Parent volunteers expand their knowledge and understanding of school programs. Children take pride in their parents' involvement in classroom activities. Volunteers promote a community understanding of school needs. Volunteers like you are important people!!!

All children are different. The quality of their work will vary.

Don't tell them they aren't interested. If they are really having trouble, this usually won't help.

Make it possible for the children to get help from each other.

Help children to see that mistakes are part of learning; they help us know what to avoid in the future.

Let children make contact with you.

Spend some extra time talking with the children when you can.

Share a child's concerns, outside interests, and new belongings.

Criticize the action, not the child, and do it privately.

Don't point out one child as the "only one" who hasn't followed directions or a rule.

When working with an individual child, try to sit at or stoop to the child's working level to get good eye contact.

Page 2: paste-up of typed message

Page 7: paste-up of typed message

Page 2: paste-up of student art added to complement typed message

Page 7: paste-up of student art added to complement typed message

Flyers for Fund-Raising Events

As a teacher, administrator, or leader of a community group, you may be called upon to coordinate advertising for a fund-raising event, such as a book sale or a bake sale. Advertising for these events can be a real chore. But imaginative, fun advertisements will attract customers and help the school or group.

Students often prepare their own ads for school benefits, especially when their efforts are directly related to the event, such as a car wash. Even as a parent, you may need to create imaginative flyers to attract customers to a neighborhood garage sale. This is a project that can be fun and rewarding.

To produce 8½" x 11" flyers, choose a suitable border and prepare your written message. Arrange and paste the border and message on your paste-up page. Have the flyers copied onto brightly colored paper.

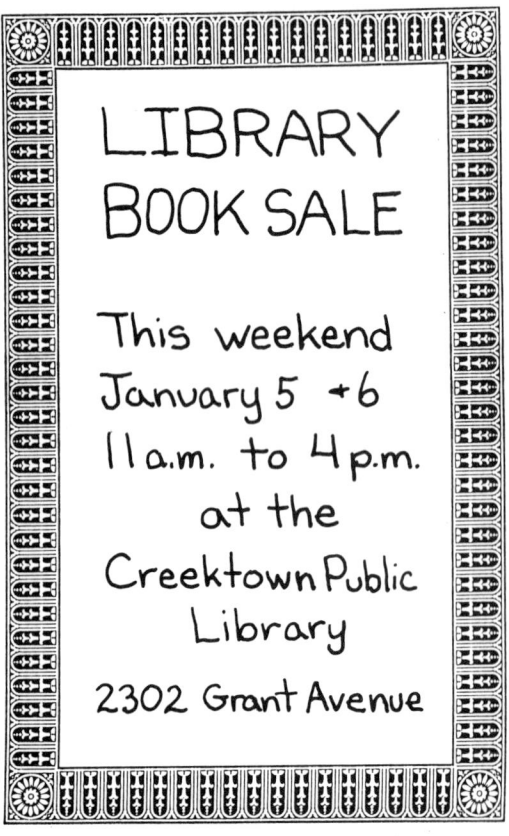

Labels and Reward Stickers

Create your own stickers! These ideas will show you how to make low-cost, self-adhesive name tags, jar labels, bookplates, and reward stickers.

Visit your copy center and ask to see the different sizes of self-adhesive labels available. Purchase one sheet to use as a paste-up sheet. If the size you want is not in stock, ask for the name of the brand and the sizes that will run through the copy center's machine. Purchase the recommended kind of label sheets at a stationery store.

Select the art and make a copy for each label on the paste-up sheet. Place the art in position on the paste-up. Have the paste-up copied onto the other label sheets. Use felt markers to add a spot of color to each sticker.

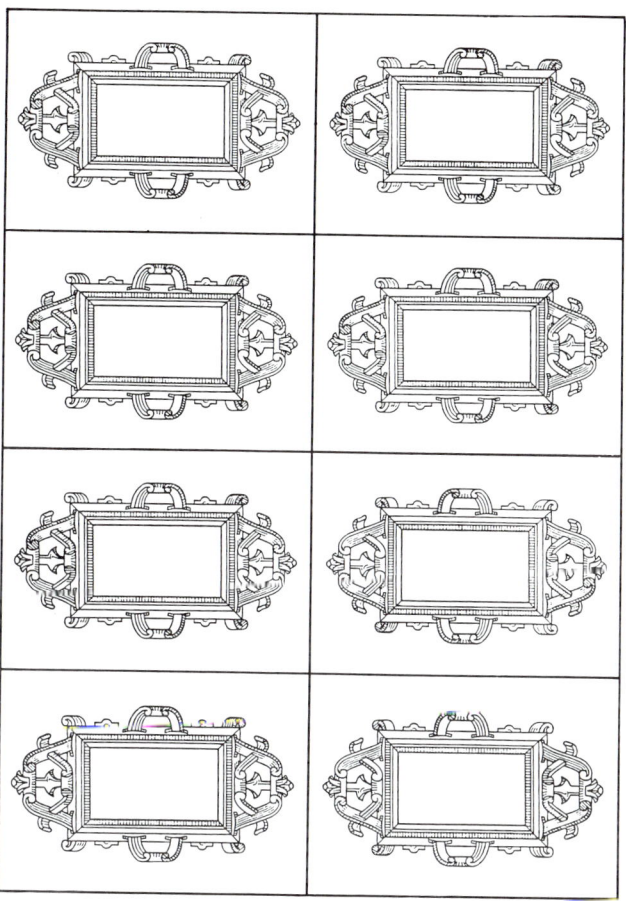

Self-Adhesive Name Tags

When you need name tags for meetings or special events, try making your own on self-adhesive label sheets. Personalize them with your group's logo or your school insignia, or use other art.

Self-Adhesive Jar Labels

Choose some line art for a jar label design and copy onto self-adhesive label sheets. You can use these stickers to label jars of supplies in your classroom. Students may enjoy making labels and decorated jars as gifts for friends and family.

Self-Adhesive Bookplates

Students can draw their own bookplate designs or select art from the back of this book. Students will enjoy designing bookplates to give as gifts, too.

Prepare the art and words for a 4¼" x 5½" bookplate. Make four copies of the completed design. Fold a standard 8½" x 11" paper into fourths, unfold it, and then paste the four copies of art in position. Have your paste-up copied onto 8½" x 11" self-adhesive sheets and cut the copies into fourths with scissors, an X-acto® knife, or a paper cutter.

Self-Adhesive Reward Stickers

Reward stickers are excellent motivators and can be designed in various shapes and sizes. If you want to create some unique shapes, have your sticker designs copied onto 8½" x 11" sheets of self-adhesive paper and cut out each sticker. To save cutting time, use the standard shapes and sizes of precut labels.

Stationery

Handmade stationery can express the artistic personality of its designer. It can also serve as a personalized gift with a design that reflects the interests and personality of the intended recipient. Having students create their own stationery may even be a way to encourage them to write letters more frequently and improve their communication skills.

Begin with the name and address. The words can be positioned at the top or bottom of the page, centered or placed on the side, stretched in one line across the width of the page or stacked in several lines. You may wish to create a design using the letters in the name or address, as shown below. Instead, you could hand-letter or use typewritten or typeset words for the name and address. Then add an original drawing or a border from the back of this book.

On a standard 8½" x 11" paper, paste the name and address and any other art in position. Have your paste-up copied the number of times that you wish.

Have the paste-up of the name and address reduced to an appropriate size (3" x 1") as a return address for a coordinating envelope. Make return address labels from your paste-up reduction and affix them to #10 (standard size 9½" x 4") envelopes. (See the section about preparing a paste-up for copying self-adhesive labels on page 25.)

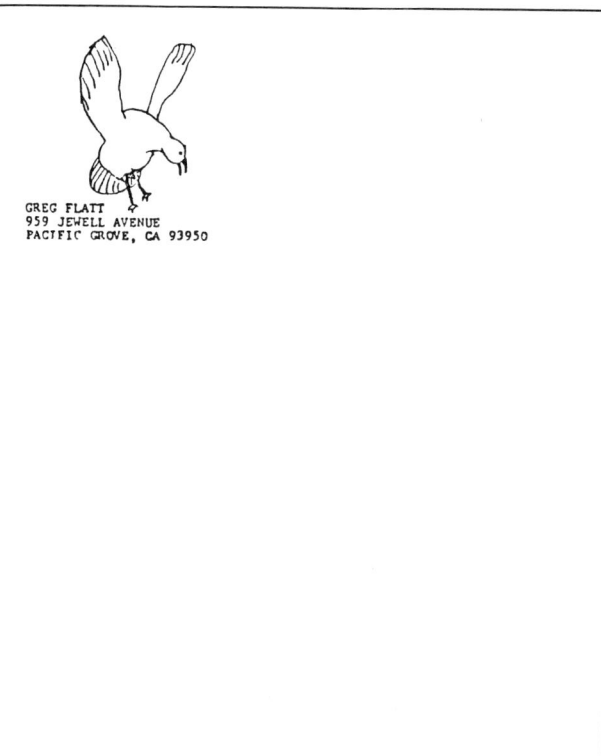

Bookmarks

Making original bookmarks is a perfect way to incorporate student drawings in an instant graphics project. It's economical, too, because one sheet of paper yields four bookmarks.

Select the art. You may also wish to add a simple message. Make four copies of the art and the message. Enlarge or reduce them if necessary.

Fold a standard 8½" x 11" paper into fourths, as shown. Unfold the paper and then paste the art in place in each of the four sections. Have your paste-up copied onto heavy card stock. Cut apart the finished bookmarks.

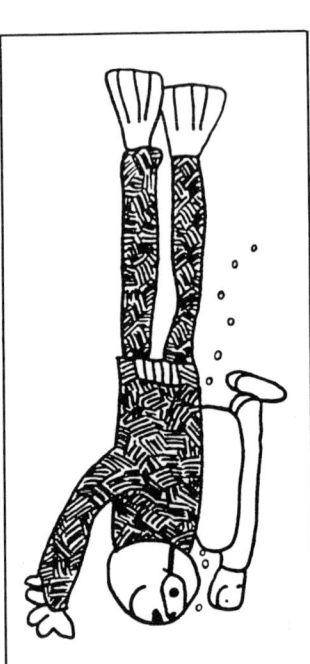

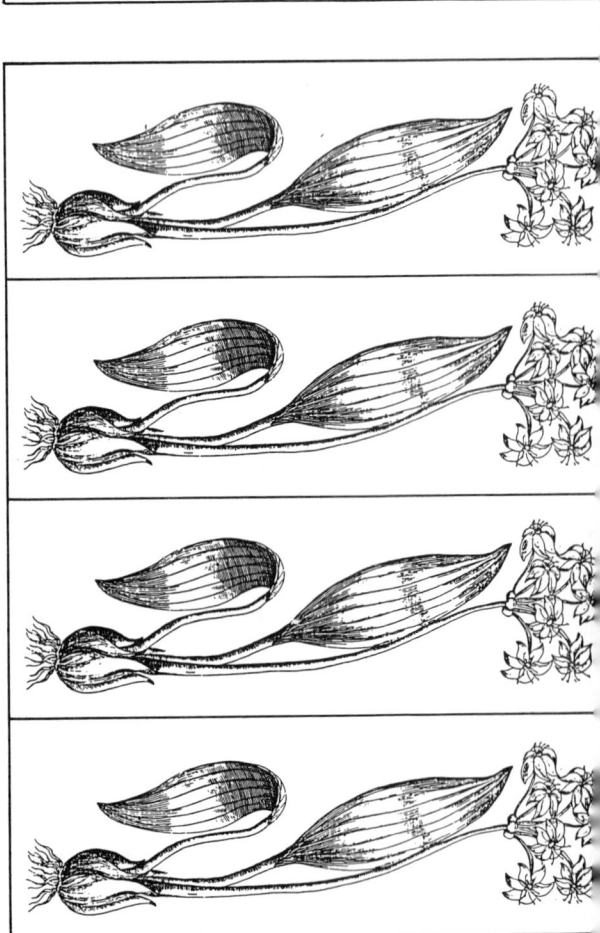

Calendar

A calendar is a fun project for the class to do after the winter holiday break. If the calendar is produced earlier in the school year, it can be used as a practical and charming item for school fund-raising campaigns. Marked with the dates of school functions, community events, and holidays, the calendar squares can also include plenty of space in which to write notes. This project can involve every class in the school. The children will enjoy seeing their art and that of their classmates each month.

Make 12 copies of the calendar grid from the back of the book. Letter the names of the months. Then number the days of the months and label the squares with any important dates, such as holidays and school activities.

Calendar grid

Paste-up of completed calendar grid

Divide the task of illustrating the cover and the pictures for the 12 months. For example, let each participating class take one illustration. Each class then selects a theme, such as Halloween, autumn, or summer vacation, to portray the assigned month. Consistency within the calendar is not necessary. However, all illustrations should be horizontal.

Paste-up of illustration for calendar month

The class illustration can be done in several ways. One approach is to give each child a small square of white paper and a fine-line black felt marker. Have the children draw in their squares and print their names beside the drawings. Paste these onto an 8½" x 11" sheet of white paper and copy the sheet. If the drawings won't fit, paste them onto a larger sheet of paper (proportionately the same as an 8½" x 11" sheet) and reduce it. Another method is to have the students make a group drawing. Using fine-line markers, each student adds his or her illustration directly to a shared piece of 8½" x 11" white paper. Other group projects, such as styrofoam tray printing or nature prints, can be adapted for calendar art. (See pages 9-10.)

You might want to draw a simple line border around the art or select an appropriate one from the back of this book. Make 12 copies. At the top, print the name of the teacher whose class prepared the art. Then paste the copy of the art done by that class in place. For the cover page, you may want to choose a different, more elaborate border and type or lettering style for the name of your school. Paste a copy of the cover border and words in position with the children's art.

Paste-up of calendar cover

To be sure that all the pages are copied in the correct order, make two copies of the art pages and the grid pages. Clip together the pages that should be copied back-to-back so that the copy center will know the sequence. Give this copy to the copy center with your paste-up. Keep a master copy for yourself.

Have the calendar copied onto card stock. Punch two holes equidistant from the center at the top of each grid page and insert plastic rings so that the pages can be turned easily as the months go by. Punch one hole centered at the bottom of each grid page so that a pushpin can be used to hang up the calendar.

32 Projects

MRS. CLARK'S CLASS

Scott L., Joey, Kenneth, Michael J., Michael O., Saeeda, Scott Mc.
Aaron, Joseph, Jaela, Abby, Ricky, Leslie, Jeni
Jaime, You, Jeremy, Alex, Evan, Adam, Jocelyn
Clark, Shannon, Alexis, Maya, Branden, Stiles, Clayton
Wendy, Sam, Miranda

January

Sunday	Monday	Tuesday	Wednesday	Thursday	Friday	Saturday
1 New Year's Day	2	3	4	5	6	7
8	9	10	11	12	13	14
15 Martin Luther King's Birthday	16	17	18 PTA Meeting	19	20	21
22	23	24	25	26	27 Science Fair	28
29	30	31				

Note Cards

Begin by selecting the art for the cards. Make two copies of the art, reducing it if necessary. Each piece should measure about 4¼″ x 5½″. The art should be drawn vertically if the card is to be folded at the side or horizontally if the fold is to be at the top.

Fold a standard 8½″ x 11″ sheet of paper into fourths. Unfold the paper and then paste the art in position as shown. If you would like a signature or logo on the back of the cards, draw or write it with a black felt marker and then paste it in place.

Have the cards copied. Cut them in half and fold them so that the art appears on the front and the logo or signature is on the back.

Paste-up of note card art with signature on back

Completed, folded note card

Projects for Holidays and Special Occasions

Special occasions demand novel ideas. In this section there are four projects keyed to holiday celebrations: invitations, postcards, menus, and holiday books.

Invitations

Sending your own specially made invitations will add to the spirit of any special occasion. If the event is related to children, drawings made by children work well as illustrations on the invitations. Other kinds of invitations can be embellished with a border, line art, a photograph, or a print project. Make one copy of each piece of art that you select.

For a full-page invitation, paste the art in place on a piece of 8½" x 11" paper. Write or type the message, including the nature of the event, date, time, and location. Have the paste-up copied onto any weight paper. To mail the invitations, simply fold each sheet horizontally in half or in thirds and then seal, address, and mail them.

For smaller invitations that open up to a message, make two cards on each 8½" x 11" sheet. Prepare art that will fit in a 4¼" x 5½" space. Make two copies of the art. Fold two standard 8½" x 11" sheets of paper into fourths and then unfold them. On one of those sheets, paste the two copies of art in the two right-hand sections made by the folds. Prepare your message for the invitation and make two copies of it. Paste the copies in the two right-hand sections of the other 8½" x 11" piece of paper. Have the art page and the message page copied back-to-back so that the art will appear on the outside and the message will appear on the inside of the card. Show the copy center worker what the end product should look like to make sure that the invitation is copied correctly. Cut the finished copies in half, fold them, and mail them in envelopes.

Picture Postcards

Postcards can be sent as birthday cards, holiday greetings, invitations, or notes to friends. Children will enjoy making postcards from a variety of materials, including original drawings, nature prints, borders, and photos.

Select the art and hand-letter any message that you may want to include on the front of the postcard. Make four copies of the art and the message.

Fold two standard 8½″ x 11″ sheets of paper into fourths and then unfold them. On one of the sheets, paste the four copies of art in position in the four sections. On the other piece of paper, use a black felt marker to draw a line down the middle of each of the four sections to separate the writing and the address areas. You may also wish to designate a place for the postage stamp and position a postcard insignia in each of the sections, as shown.

Have your two paste-ups copied back-to-back on card stock. Be sure to explain how the finished product should look. Cut the copies into four separate postcards.

Have these two paste-ups copied back-to-back.

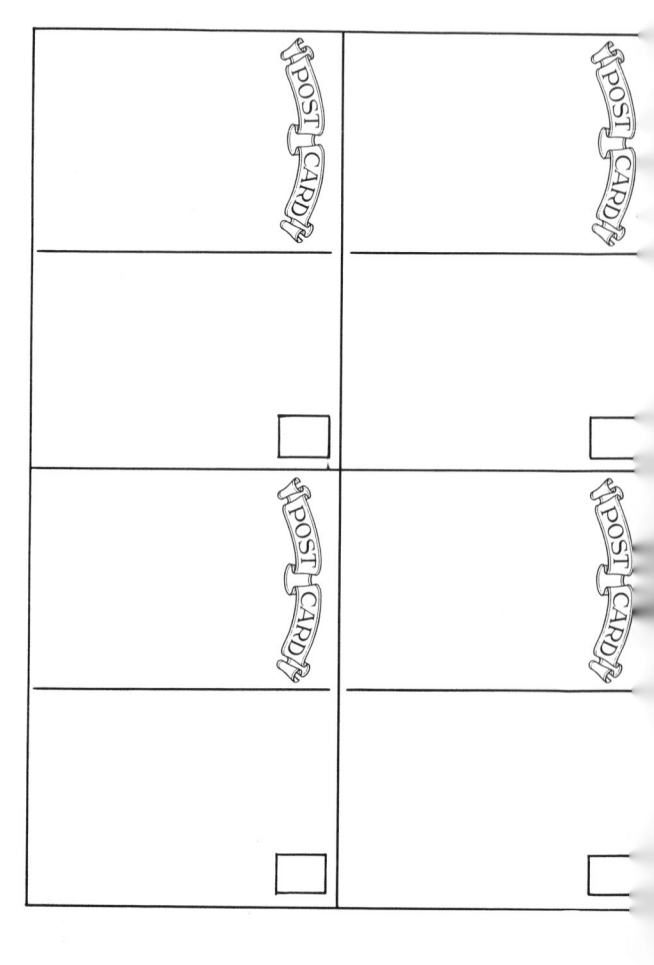

Menus

Make your own attractive menus for the school cafeteria, for special feasts or parties held at school, or for meetings or community events that include lunch or dinner. Select a border design from the back of this book. Plan your message, listing meal items and any other information. Letter the menu and make one copy of both the border and the written portion, reduced to fit within the border if necessary.

On a standard 8½" x 11" sheet of paper, paste the copy of the border in place. Then paste the copy of the written menu inside the border. Have the appropriate number of copies made. Add color to the menus with felt markers if you wish.

Paste-up of border

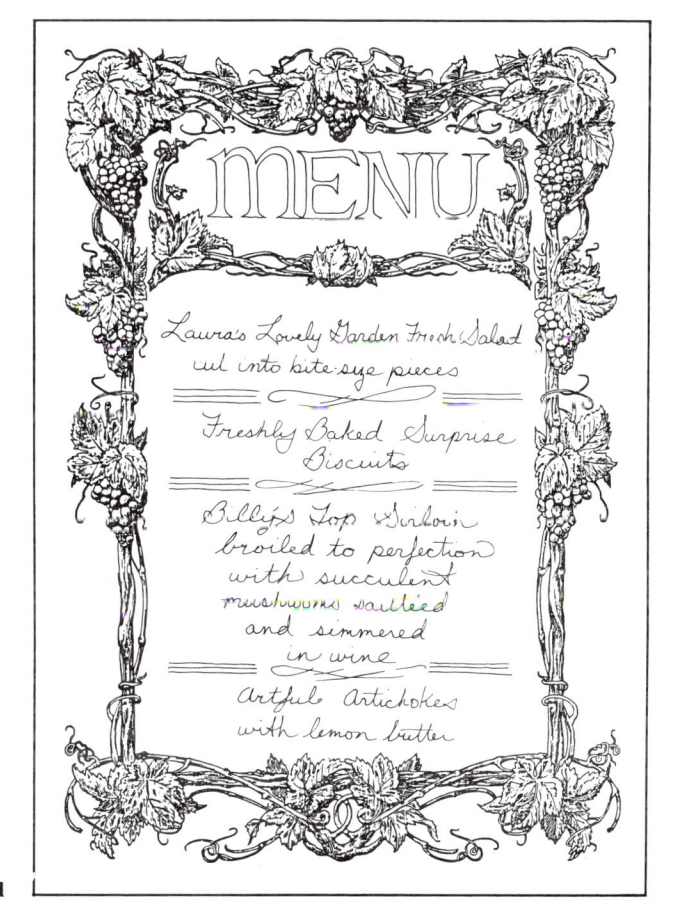

Paste-up of border with written portion of menu added

Holiday Book

A delightful way to record holiday memories and start a family or classroom tradition is to make a holiday book. Fill most of the book with pages that are blank except for a decorative border. Use these blank pages to keep recipes, photos, articles, special mementos, and any holiday-related items that you may want to collect and cherish over the years. You may also wish to include pages with copies of poems or stories in the holiday book. Children can share and illustrate these poems and stories. Make a holiday book for your own use or put together a classroom holiday book and get the students involved in the project. The students can also make holiday books for their families.

Paste-up of cover

Paste-up of blank page with border

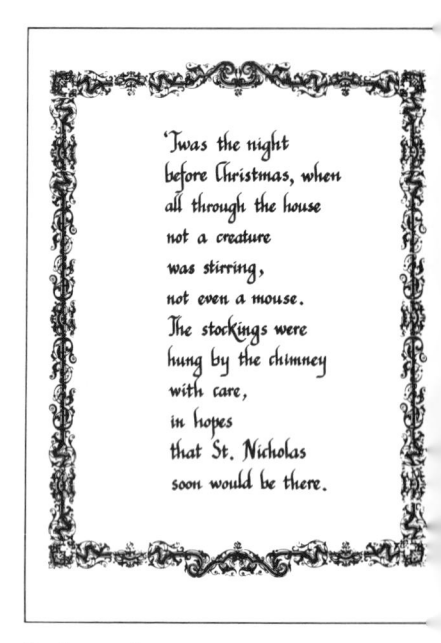

Paste-up of poem and border

From the back of this book, select a border for the 8½" x 11" pages. Make as many copies of the border as needed—one to make the paste-up for the blank pages and one for the paste-up of each poem or story you wish to include. Paste each border in place on a blank page. Then for each holiday story or poem, paste a copy of the text inside a border. Select another piece of art for the cover, letter the title, and prepare the cover page paste-up.

Have the cover page paste-up copied onto heavy-stock paper of any color. Have the paste-ups for the interior pages copied back-to-back on regular weight paper. Assemble the book and bind it. (See the description of binding techniques on page 41.)

Creative Language Arts Projects

These projects present creative and motivating ways for students to practice such language skills as vocabulary building and report writing. In addition, some projects involve sharing poetry and writing stories, thereby enriching the students' use of language. There are seven different Creative Language Arts projects: a classroom newspaper, study unit booklets, fingerprint stories, vocabulary posters, poetry posters, stand-up cards for report writing, and thematic writing paper.

Classroom Newspaper

A fun way to extend writing skills is to have each student contribute an article to a class newspaper. A newspaper is a good way to document the many interesting, valuable events that occur in the classroom, as well as the topics that engage students' attention. It also provides a means of communicating to parents, faculty, and students in other classrooms.

Let the students decide on the topics to be included. Assign or have each student select a subject and, as a "reporter," write about it. Type the articles to fit the width of the columns. (Choose a format based on the grade level, skills, and interests of your students.) Have the students illustrate their articles, using fine-line black felt markers and pieces of paper sized to fit the space available. (Some preliminary layout, therefore, will be necessary.) Consider letting the students share the writing and illustrating tasks.

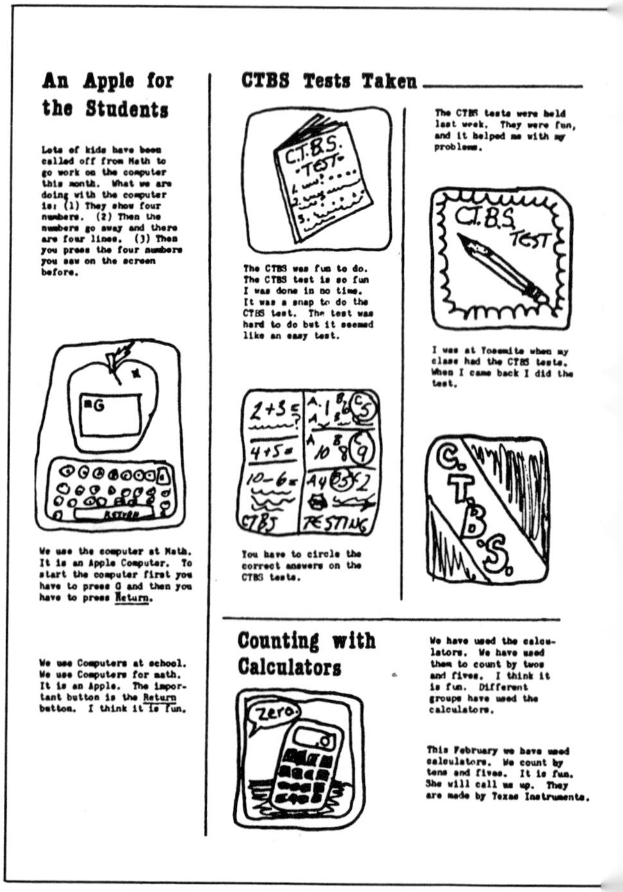

Copy a masthead or frame for the newspaper title from the back of this book. Letter the title and the headings for the articles. Paste the title of the newspaper in place on 8½" x 11" paper. Use a black felt marker to draw the column rules. Arrange the headings, typed articles, and illustrations, and paste them in place. Have the paste-ups copied back-to-back. If the newspaper runs more than two pages, staple the pages together.

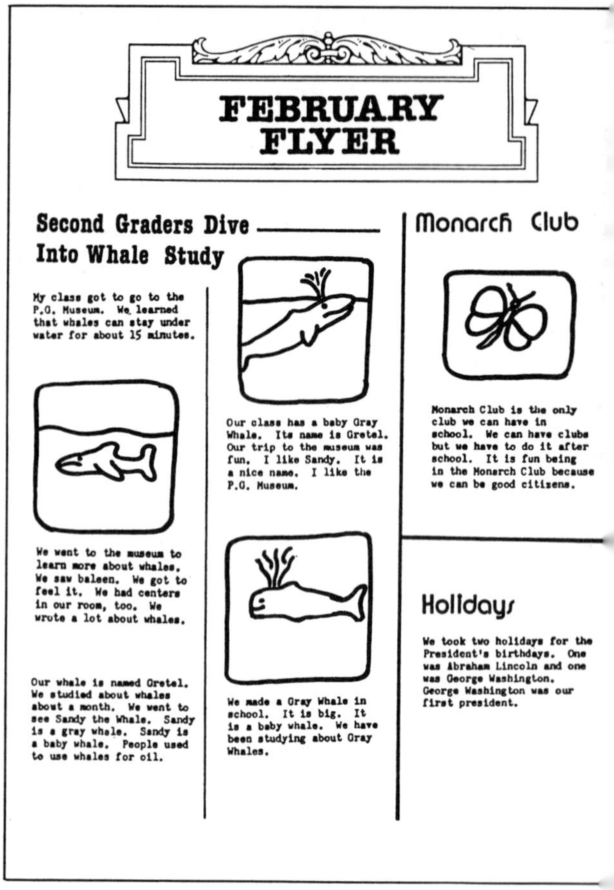

Study Unit Booklets

As a culminating activity for a special area of the curriculum, have students make study unit booklets. The booklets allow students to demonstrate what they have learned and to participate in a group effort. In addition, the project gives parents an opportunity to appreciate the extent of the study unit and the scope of their children's ideas.

You can make the booklets any size. However, the technique described here is for an 8½" x 11" format copied on one side of a page. You may wish to make smaller or larger booklets and use two-sided copying. Apply a variety of art techniques, from drawing to printing. A few different techniques are shown in the illustrations taken from pages in sample booklets.

There are several different methods for binding the booklets. See the illustrations below. Choose an appropriate method. You can bind booklets on the top or at the side. Have students prepare their pages either horizontally or vertically and bind the booklets accordingly.

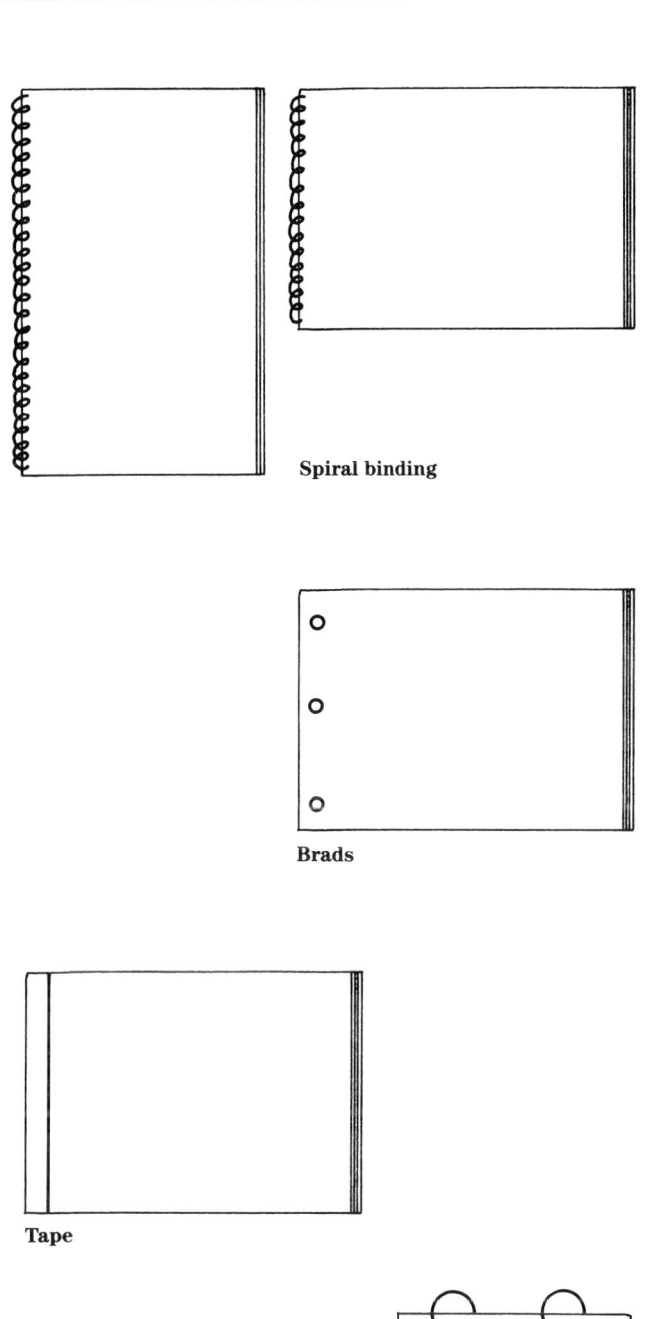

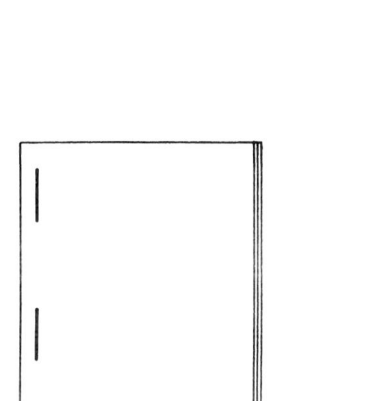

Spiral binding

Brads

Tape

Rings

Staples

To save paper, have the pages printed on both sides. (See the paste-up directions for two-sided copying on pages 22-23.) If the pages are numbered or the booklet is arranged in sequential order, prepare a mock-up of the booklet. (Refer to pages 22-23 for preparing a mock-up.) Following are a few sample pages taken from study unit booklets produced by students.

Dinosaur Booklet

For this booklet, students used the styrofoam tray printing method. Pictures accompanied the students' written reports about dinosaurs. The reports were presented in the students' own handwriting. The teacher provided writing paper with guidelines drawn in non-reproducible blue pencil. The students wrote or printed with black felt markers.

Volcano Booklet

This booklet emphasized vocabulary words and required students to draw their own versions of scientific diagrams. This illustration shows a drawing that was chosen for a booklet cover. To avoid excessive repetition, the teacher provided a vocabulary list and different subtopics within the main subject, each of which focused on a few words from the list.

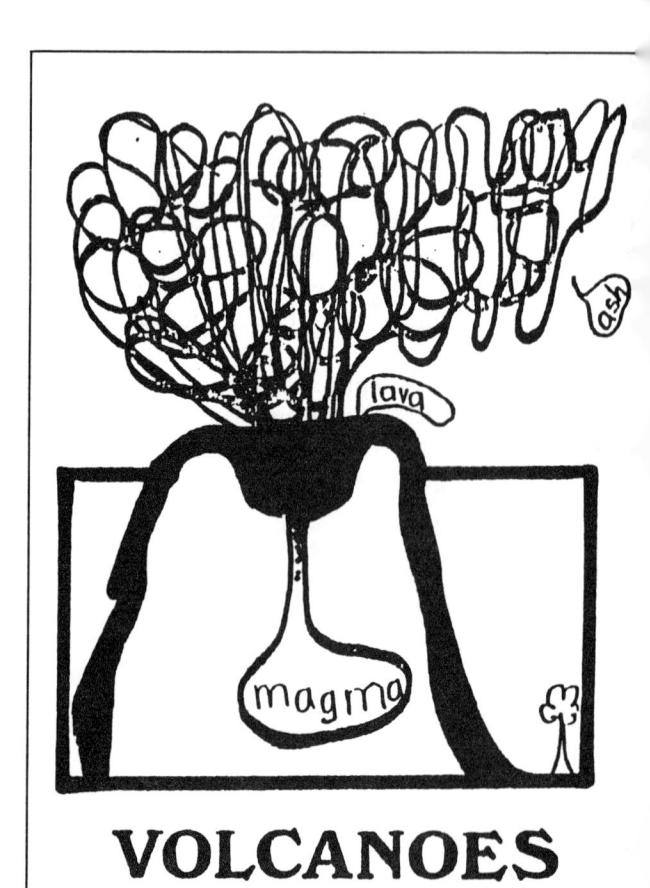

Quilt Block Booklet

This study of quilts provided an interdisciplinary lesson in history, art, textiles, and geometric math. After studying quilts, each student designed a quilt block using graph paper and a black felt marker. This booklet would also make a great coloring book.

ABC Booklet

This booklet was used to help young children review initial sounds. Each student selected one or two letters of the alphabet and drew objects that began with those letters. The teacher provided alphabet pages (copies of paste-ups that were prepared beforehand). You could use decorative letters from the back of this book to make alphabet pages.

Fingerprint Stories

Supply a stamp pad, plain white paper, and fine-line black felt markers. Have the students make fingerprint drawings. First, they can press their fingers and thumbs on the ink pad and make prints on the paper. After the ink dries, they can create cartoonlike characters from their own fingerprints with felt markers.

Provide paper with lines spaced appropriately for the students' writing abilities. The students will choose their favorite fingerprint characters, cut them out (leaving some white space around each one), and add them to the lined paper. Then they can free their imaginations to write stories about their characters.

You may wish to compile the stories in a booklet. (See the direction for making a handbook on pages 22–23 and the description of binding techniques on page 41.)

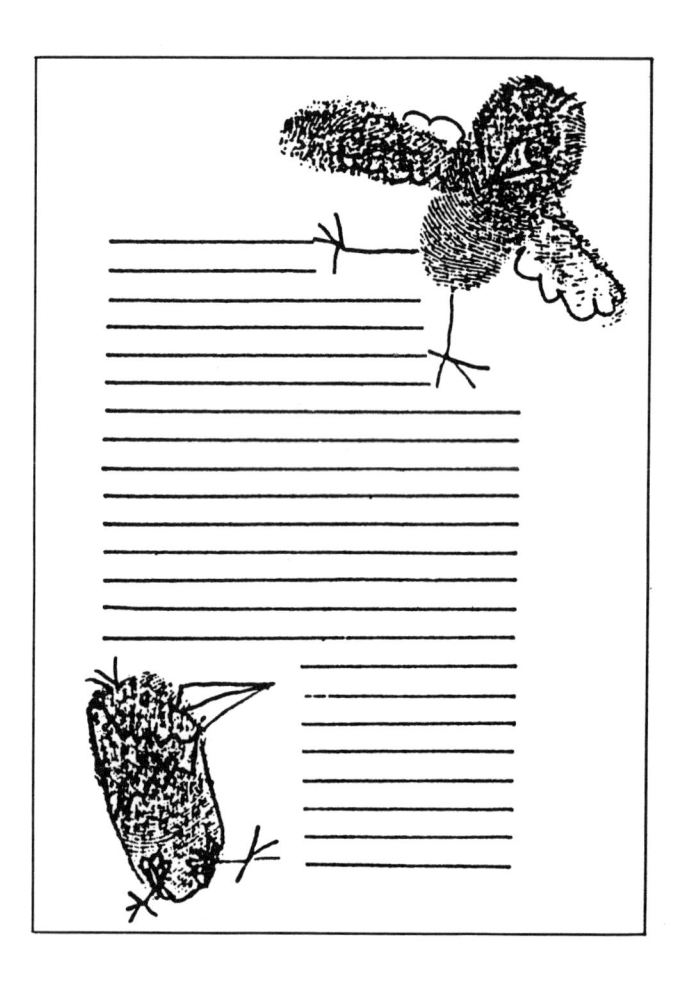

Vocabulary Posters

Emphasize vocabulary words from a special study unit by making a vocabulary poster, complete with student art. This project is appropriate for any grade level and any area of the curriculum.

Begin by drawing a grid with a black felt marker on 8½" x 11" paper or 8½" x 14" paper. The number of grid spaces should equal the number of words in your vocabulary list. Paste the vocabulary words and the title of the poster in place.

Give each student a small piece of white paper and a fine-line black felt marker. Either assign or ask each student to choose a word to illustrate. If the drawings don't fit on the poster paper, paste them onto a background paper (sized proportionately to the poster dimensions) and copy them, reducing the page to the appropriate size.

Paste the students' art in the grid spaces. You may also wish to write each student's name beside his or her piece of art. Have the paste-up of the poster copied onto regular weight paper or card stock.

Poetry Poster

Poetry posters can be designed with ease and can combine student art with poetry appreciation. This poster is formatted for 8½" x 11" paper, but you can use longer paper. Allow students to share their favorite poems. Let them create their own posters by choosing or writing the poems, illustrating the poems, and preparing the paste-ups. This preparation includes hand-lettering the poem and arranging the illustration to fit the text.

Select a poem to be highlighted on a class poster. Hand-letter or type the text of the poem. Then give each student a small piece of white paper and a fine-line black felt marker. Have them draw pictures that relate to the poem and print their names beside their pictures. Reduce the drawings to fit the poster design, if necessary. Arrange the students' drawings and the copy of the poem on an 8½" x 11" sheet of paper. Have the poster copied onto card stock.

Jack-o-lantern

I'll carve a mouth
So big and wide.
I'll carve two eyes
Side by side.
I'll carve a nose—
Oh, what a sight!—
To frighten everyone
On Halloween night.

Stand-up Cards for Report Writing

To emphasize a specific topic of study in the curriculum, have students present brief informative facts on stand-up cards. Prepare these cards to motivate report writing. Or let the students design their own cards. Use these instructions to guide them.

Begin by folding a standard 8½" x 11" piece of paper in half horizontally. Draw composition lines on the lower third of the paper. Locate line art or draw original art less than 4" wide to illustrate the curriculum topic. Prepare the title. Copy the line art and the title.

Paste the copies of the art and title in position on the lined paper. The art should be placed directly on the fold so that half of it is above the fold and half is below. Have this paste-up copied onto card stock.

Place the cards flat on the table. With an X-acto® knife, cut around the top portion of the art. Have the students write their information on the lines provided and fold the cards in half. The cut will allow the figure to stand up when the card is folded.

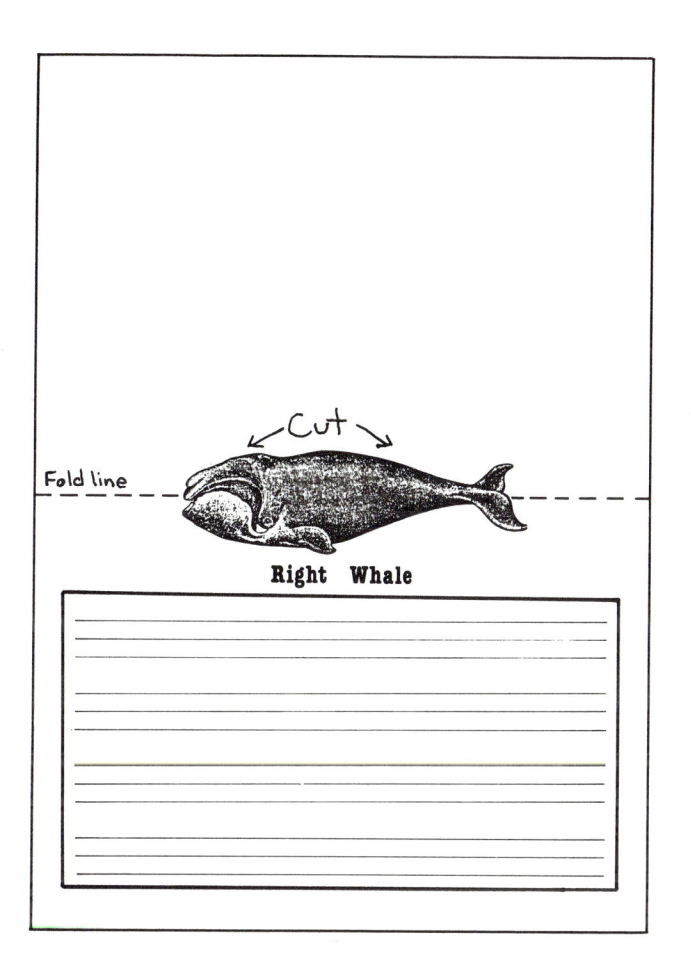

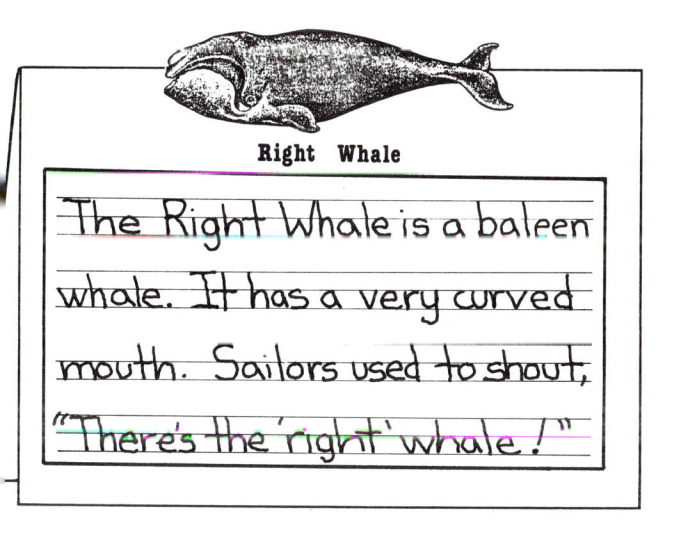

Thematic Writing Paper

When students write reports, creative stories, or poems, provide specially designed paper that matches the theme of the written project. Students may even want to design and create their own thematic paper for an assigned report or story. Special paper can often provide an added incentive for students to write, regardless of the students' grade level.

Select line art and copy each piece. Cut around the copied art, leaving at least a ¼" border. On 8½" x 11" paper, draw composition lines with a black felt marker. Determine the spacing between the lines by the grade level and writing abilities of your students. Paste the art on the paper, partially covering some of the lines. Have your paste-up copied, and you are ready to introduce the lesson!

Chapter III

Line Art
And
Headings

Instant Graphics reproducible page, copyright© 1984

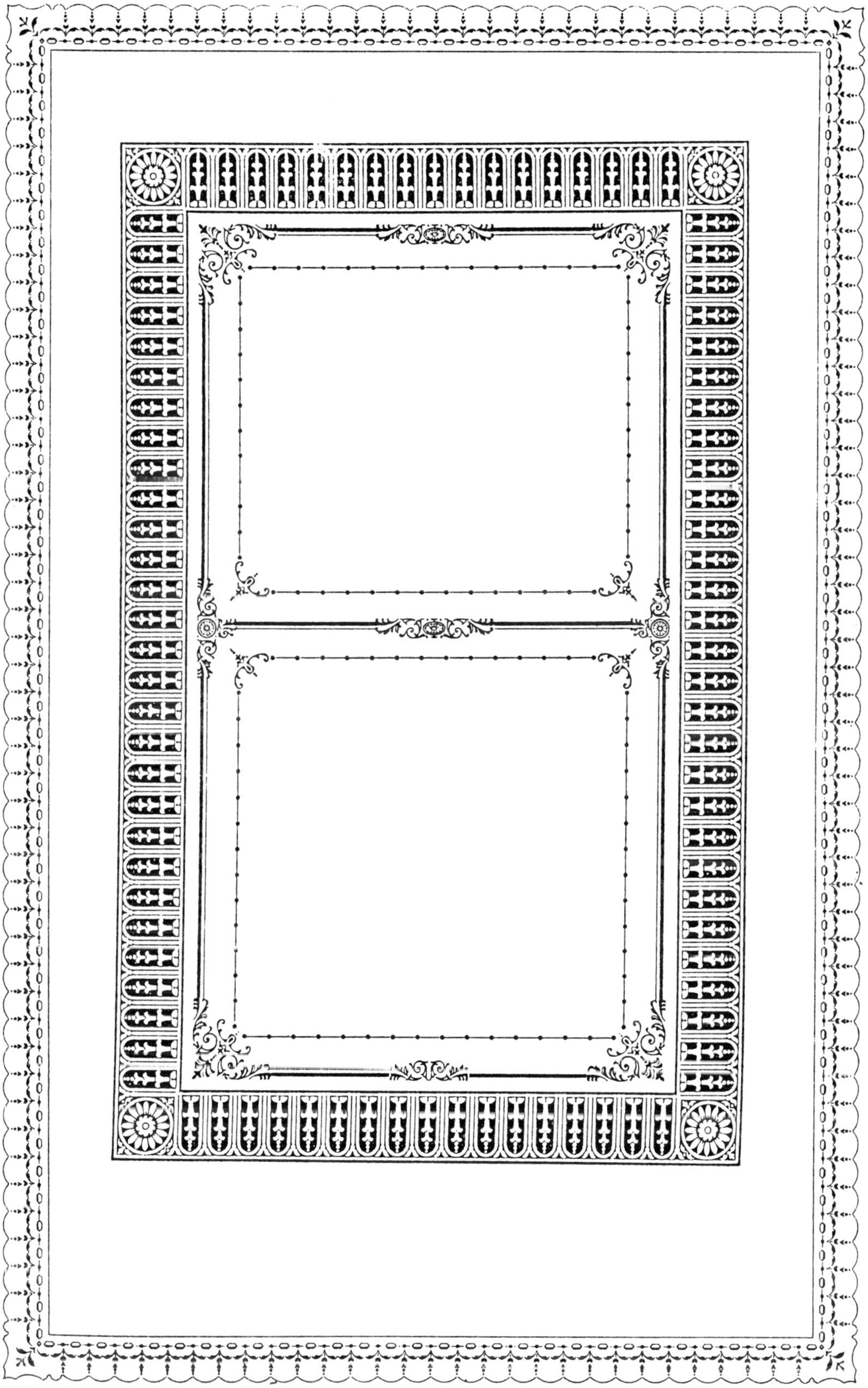

stant Graphics reproducible page, copyright© 1984

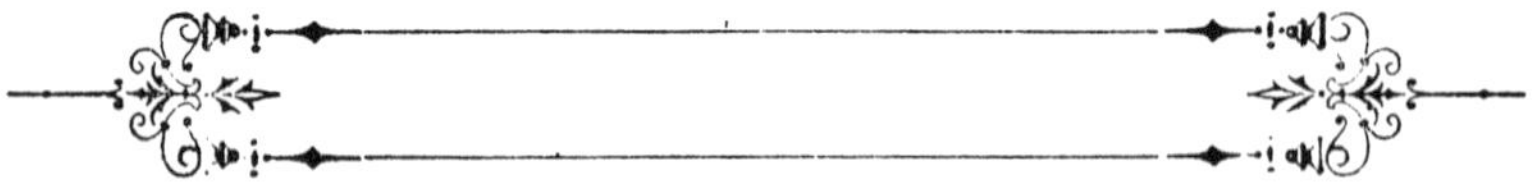

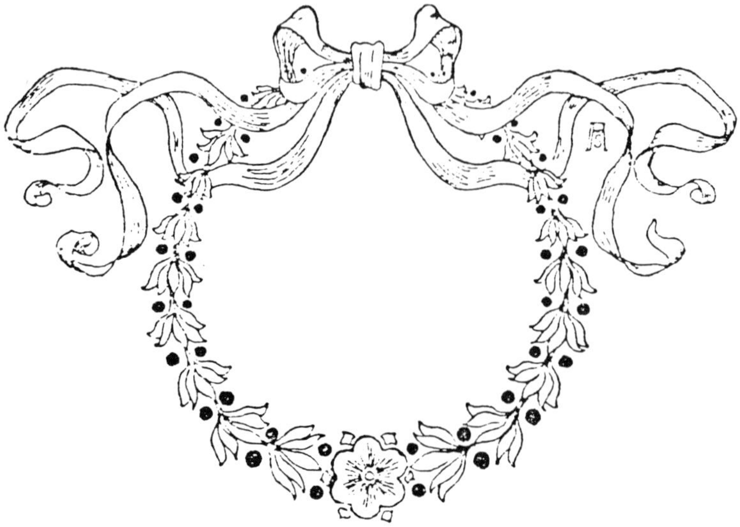

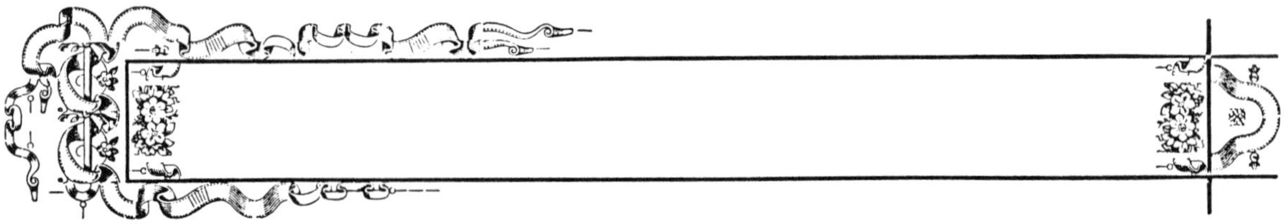

Instant Graphics reproducible page, copyright© 1984

ant Graphics reproducible page, copyright© 1984

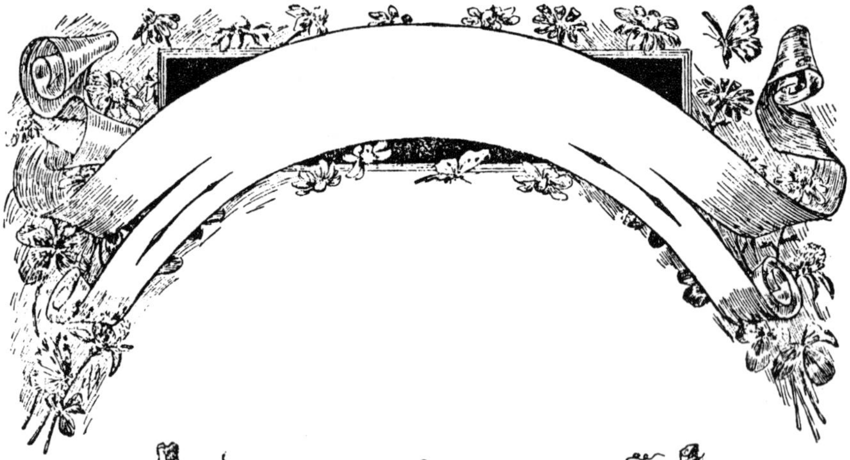

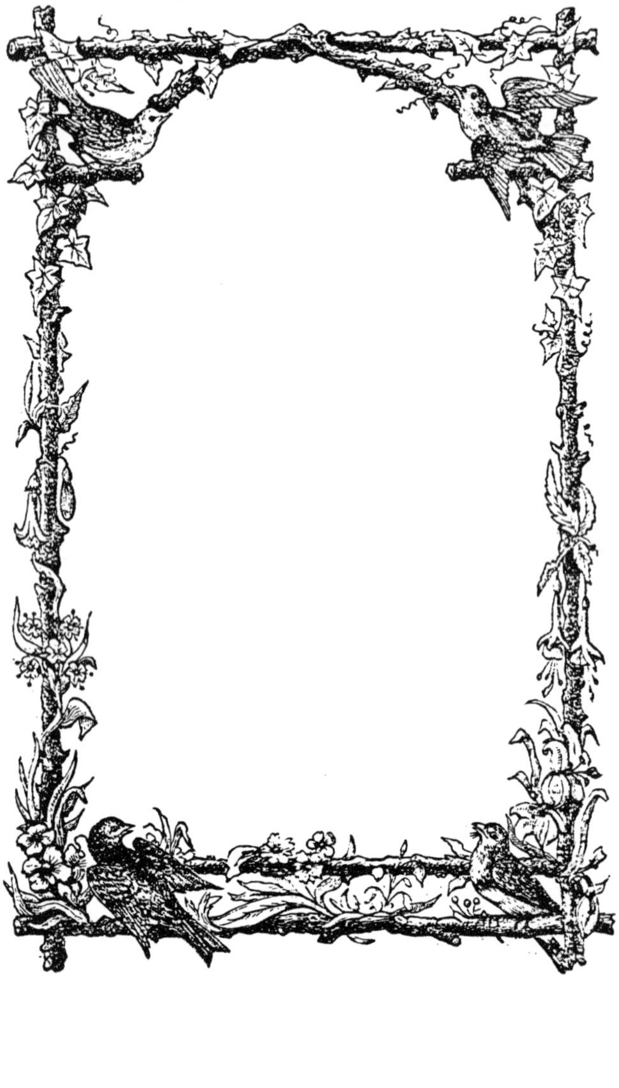

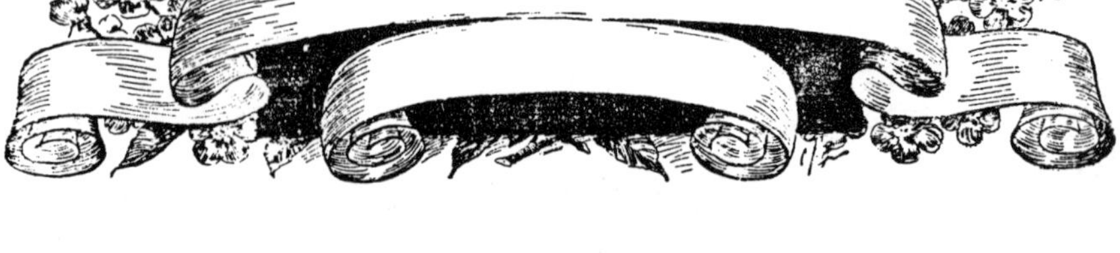

Instant Graphics reproducible page, copyright© 1984

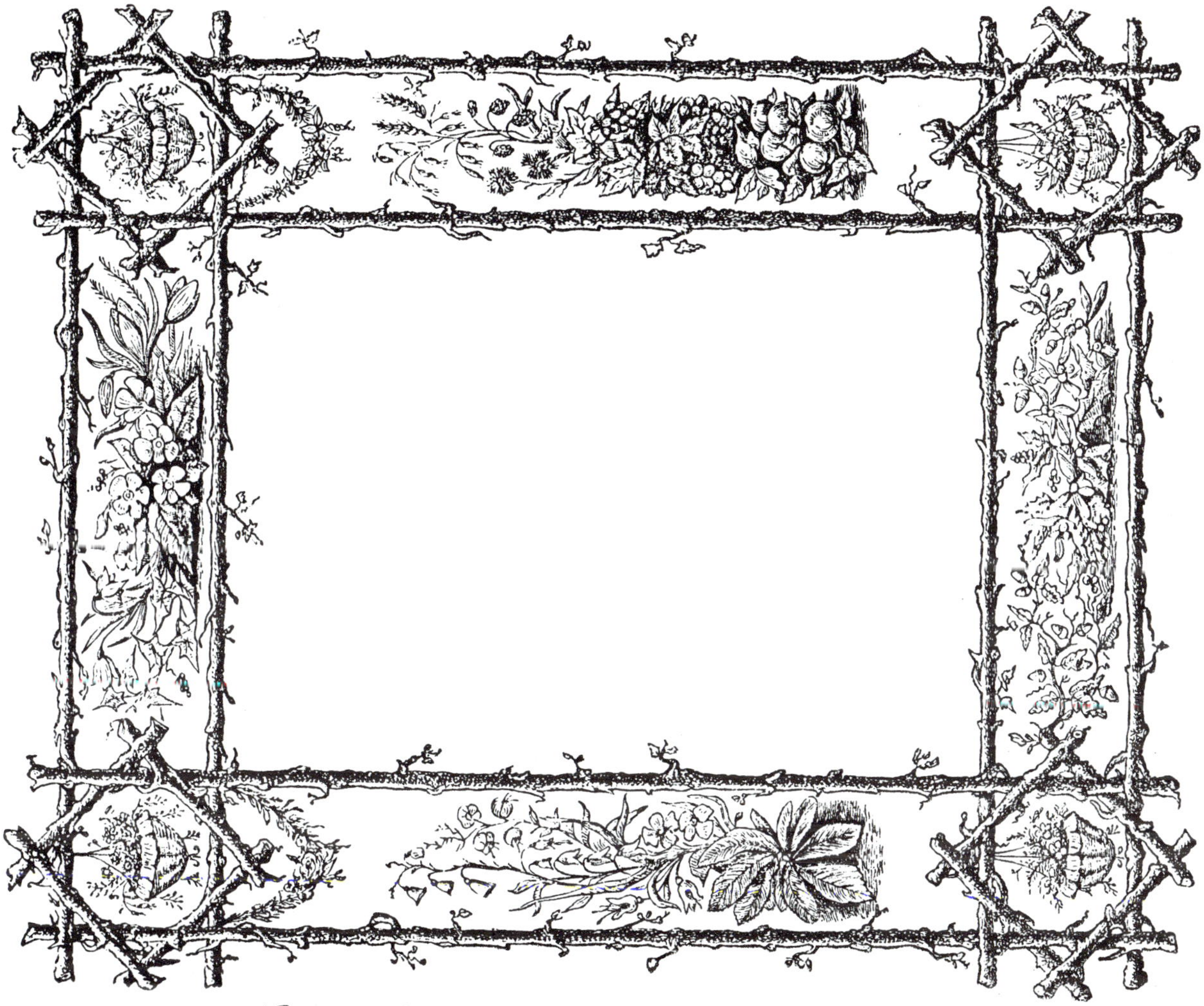

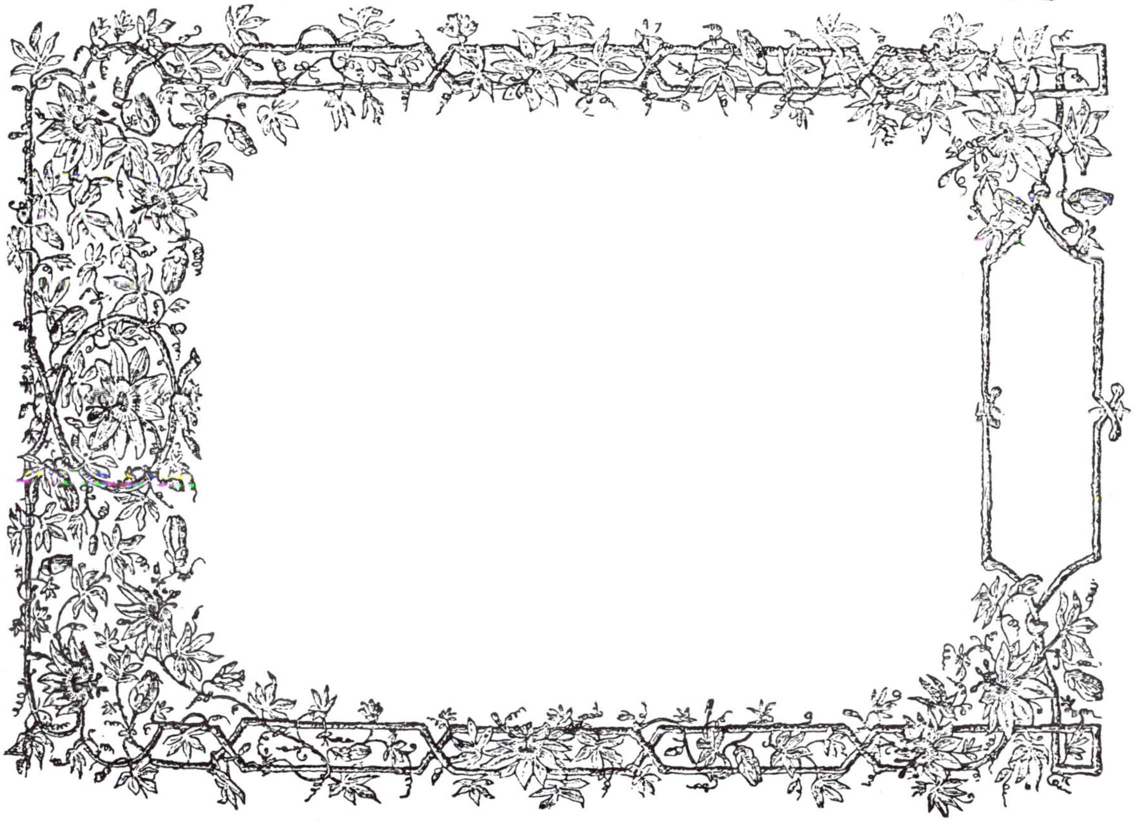

ant Graphics reproducible page, copyright© 1984

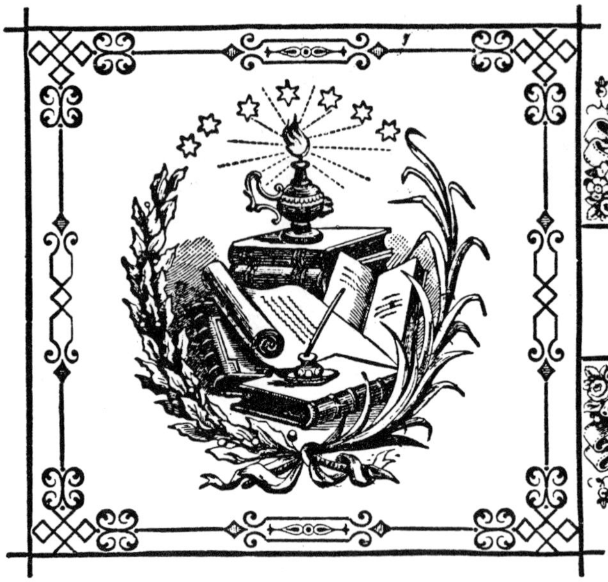

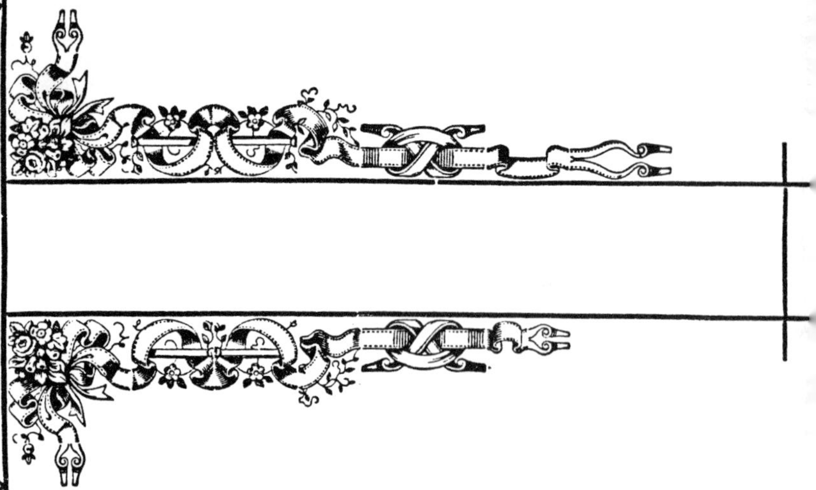

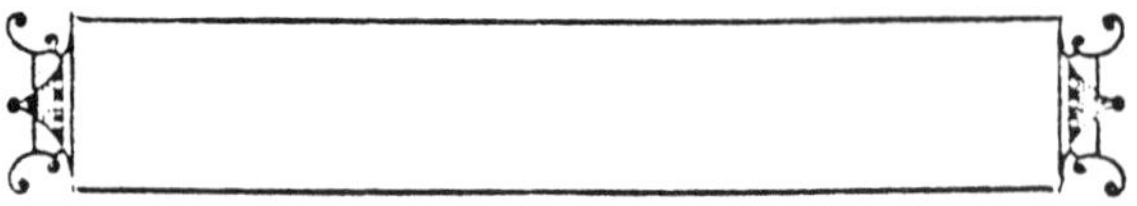

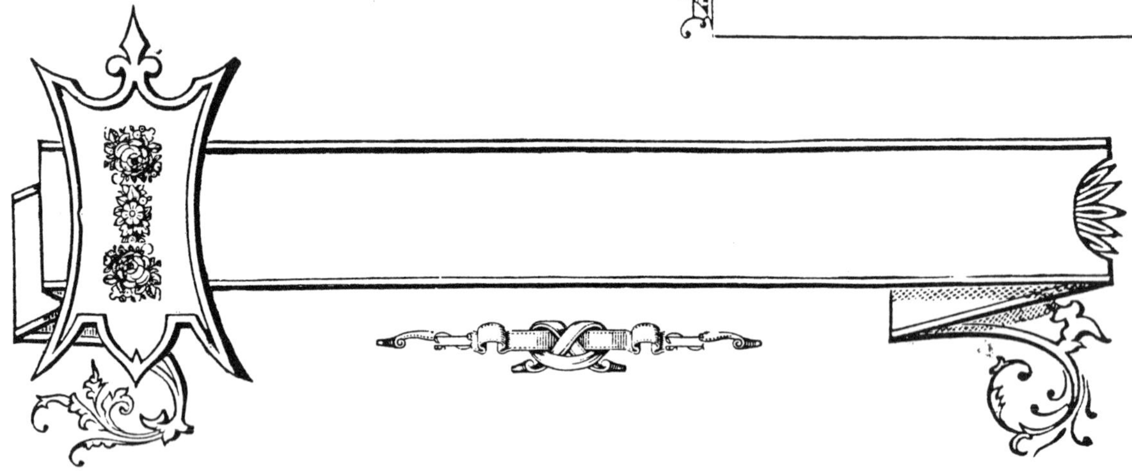

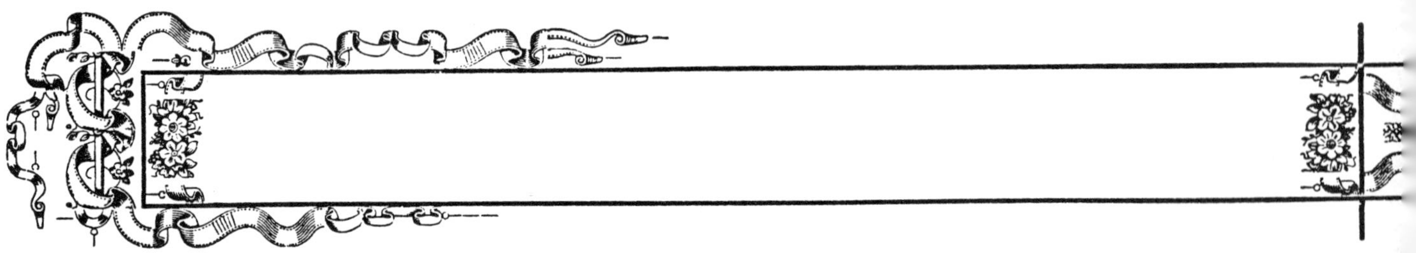

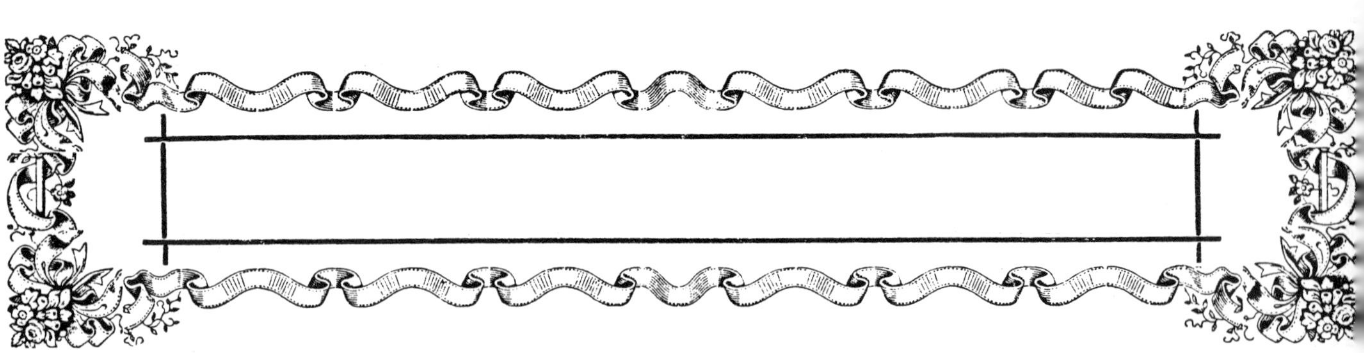

Instant Graphics reproducible page, copyright© 1984

57

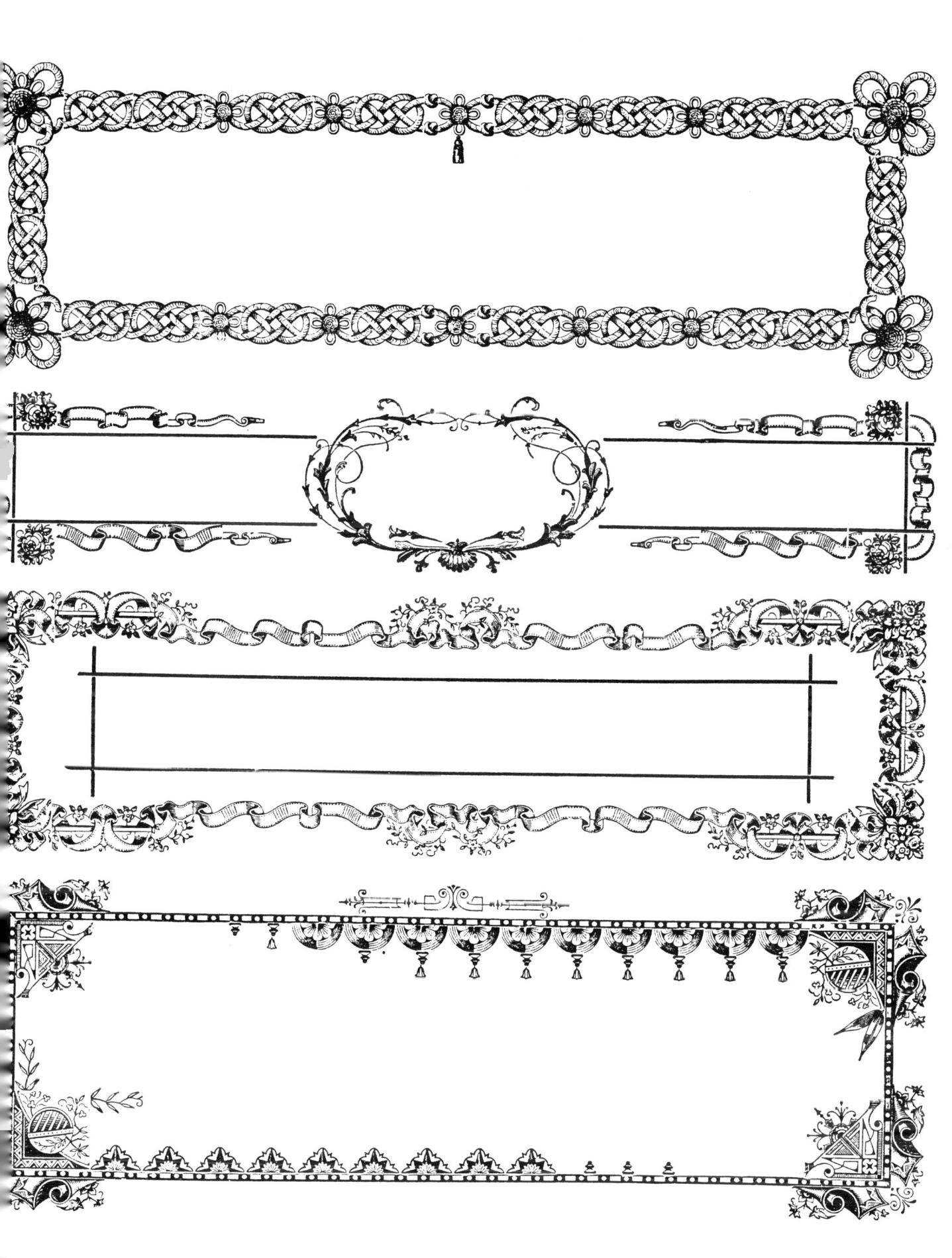

58

Instant Graphics reproducible page, copyright© 1984

59

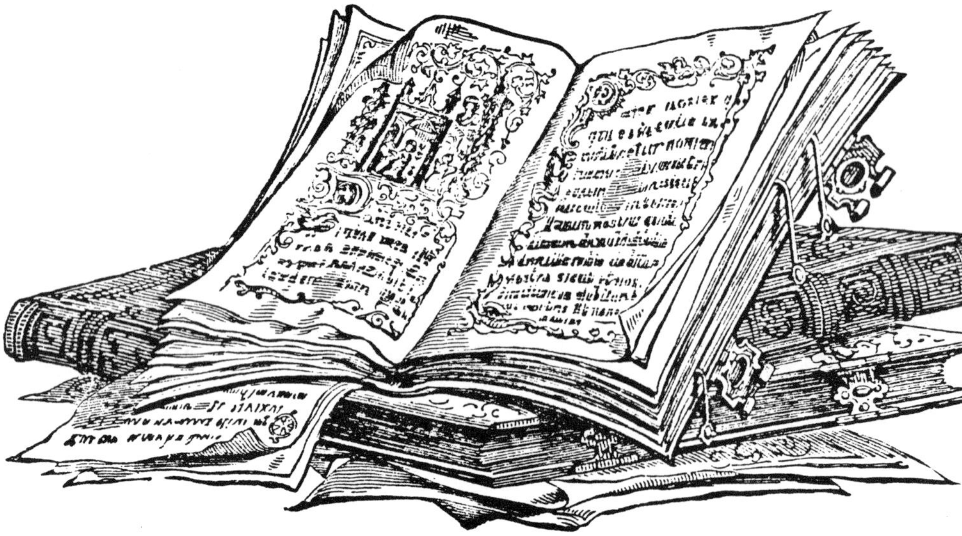

Instant Graphics reproducible page, copyright© 1984

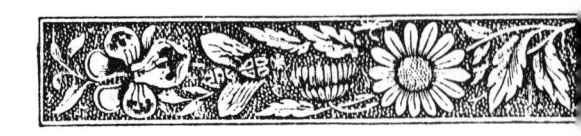

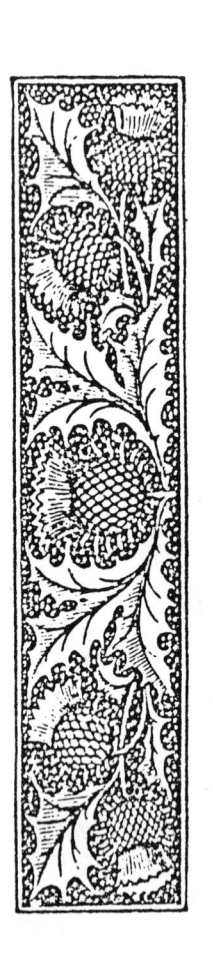

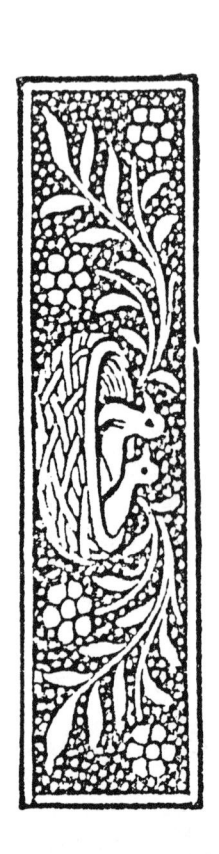

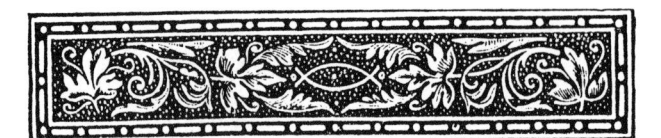

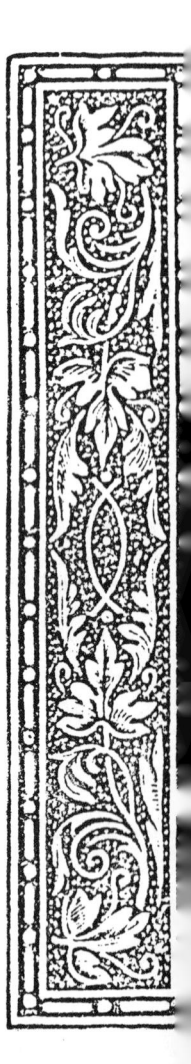

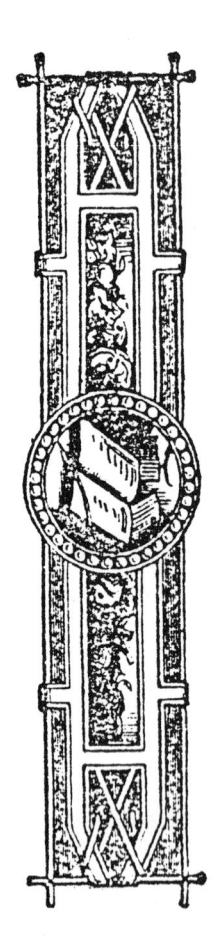

61

Instant Graphics reproducible page, copyright© 1984

63

Instant Graphics reproducible page, copyright© 1984

65

Instant Graphics reproducible page, copyright© 1984

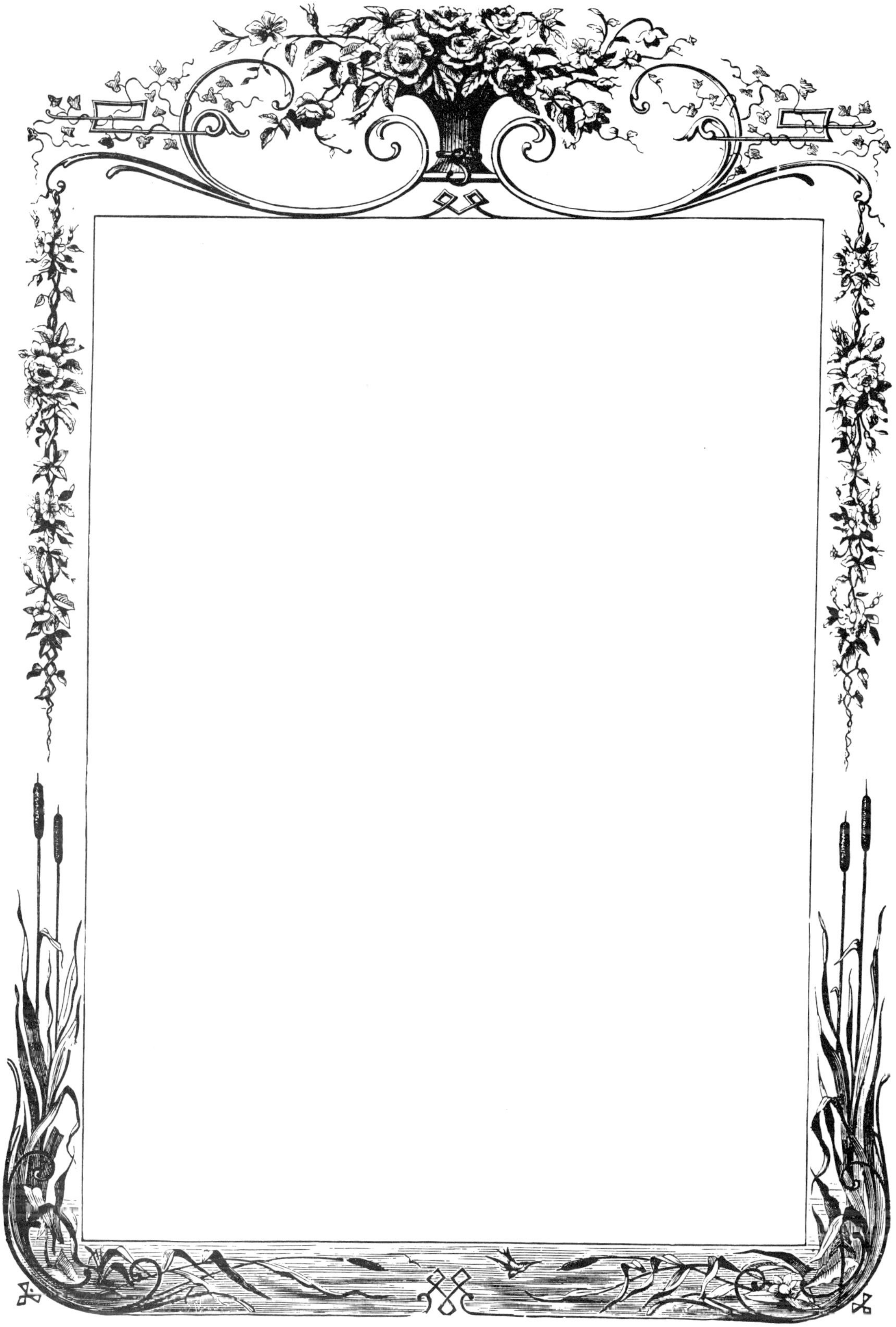

ant Graphics reproducible page, copyright© 1984

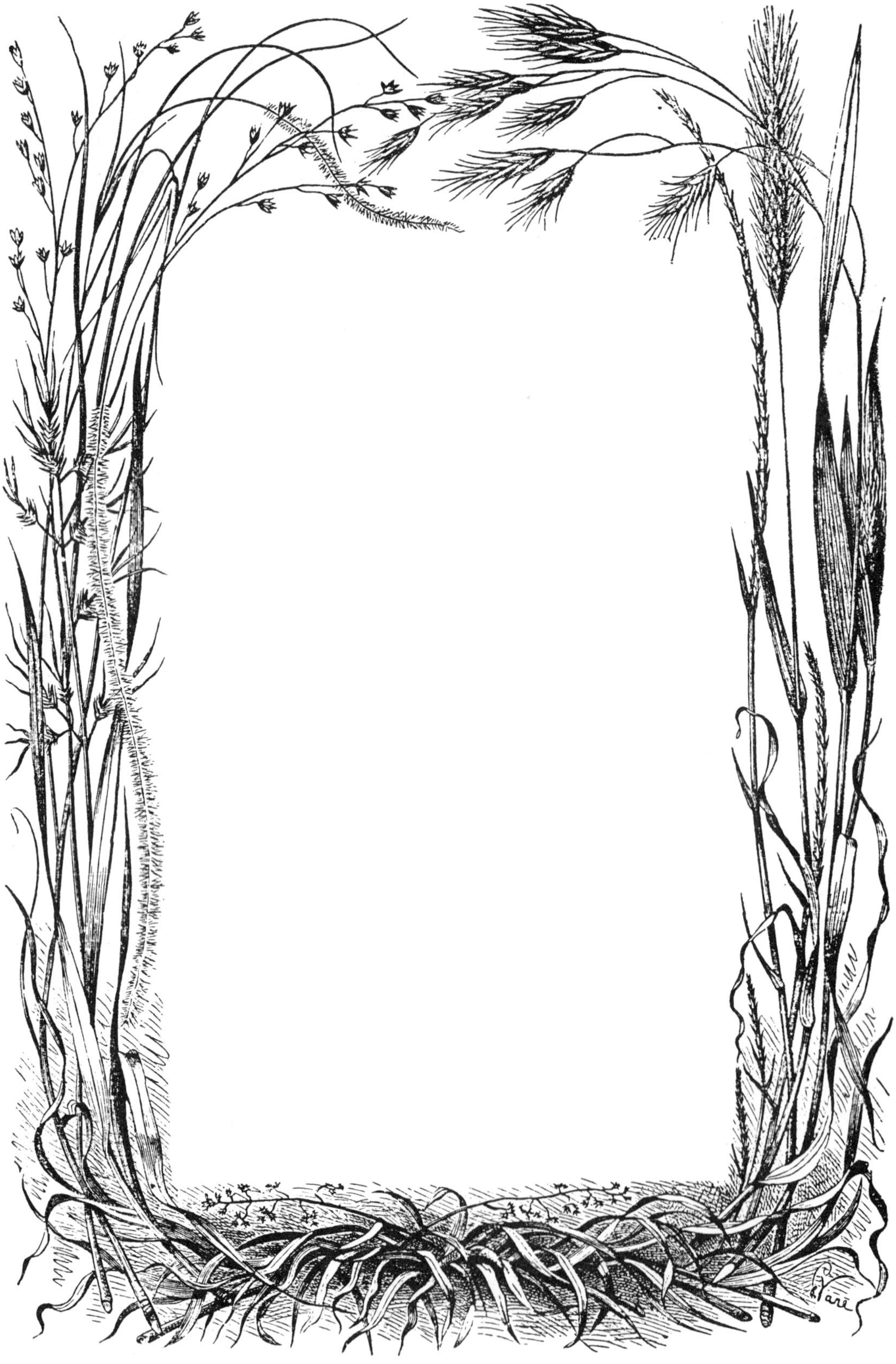

Instant Graphics reproducible page, copyright© 1984

69

Instant Graphics reproducible page, copyright© 1984

71

Instant Graphics reproducible page, copyright© 1984

73

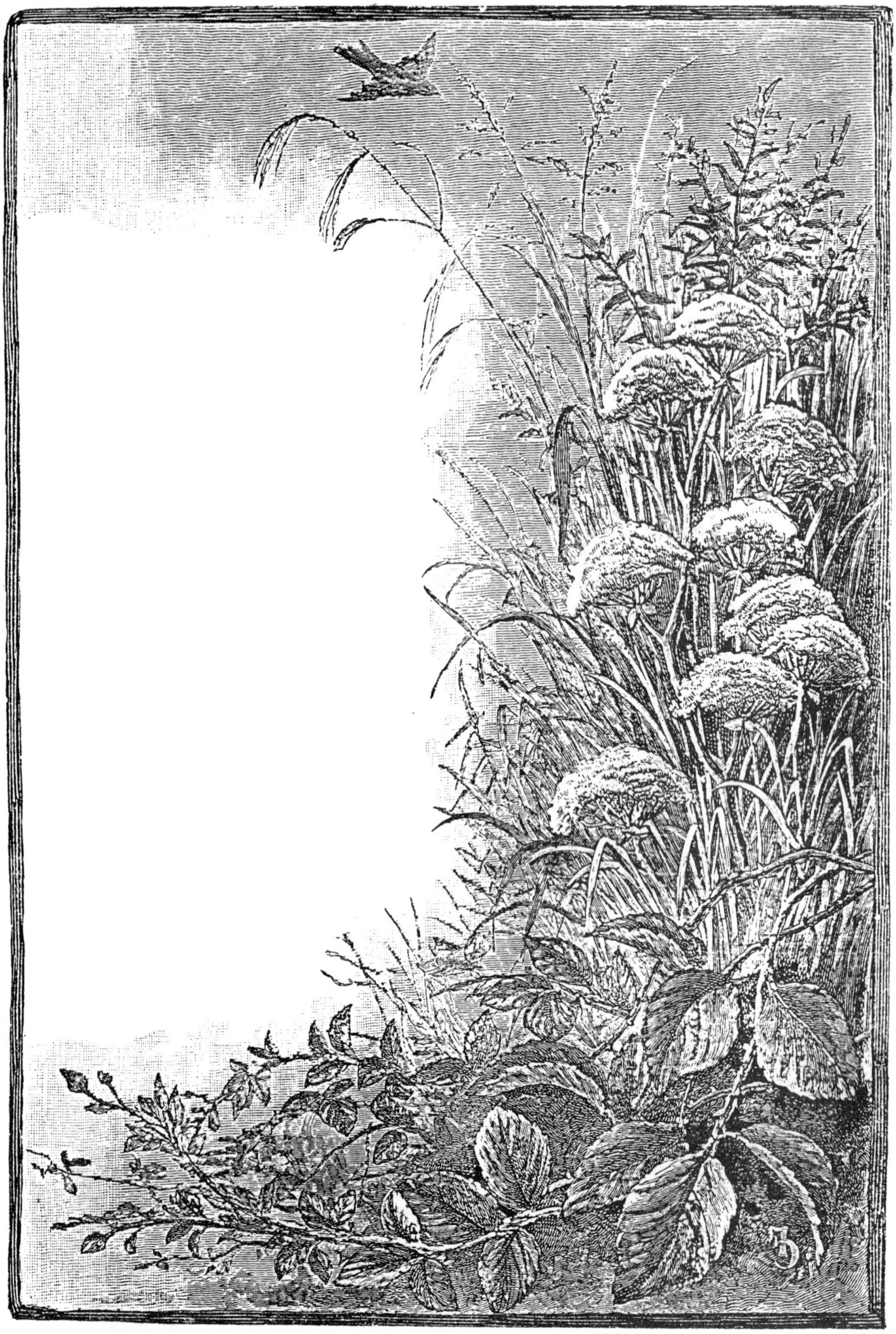

Instant Graphics reproducible page, copyright© 1984

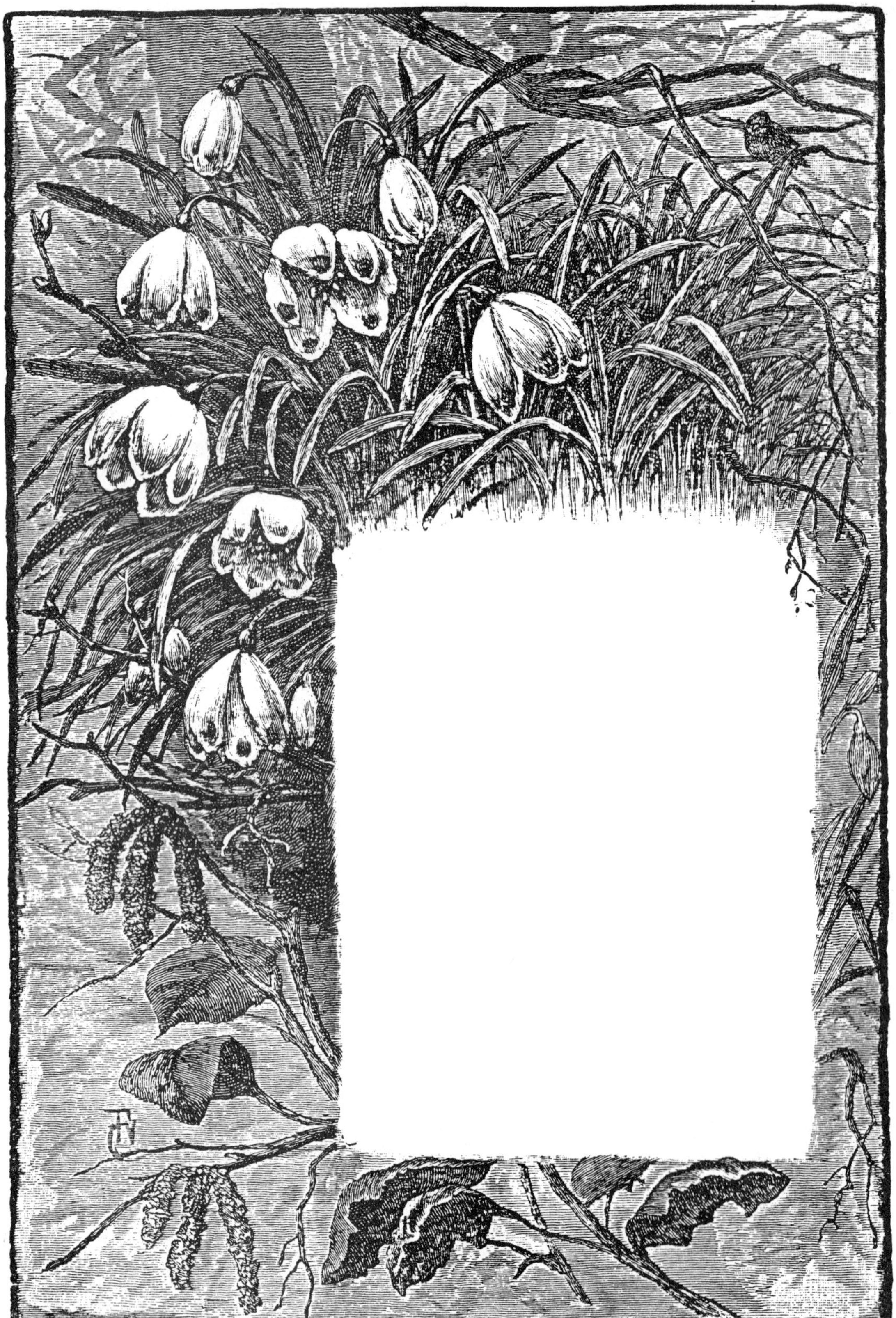

Instant Graphics reproducible page, copyright© 1984

77

Instant Graphics reproducible page, copyright© 1984

79

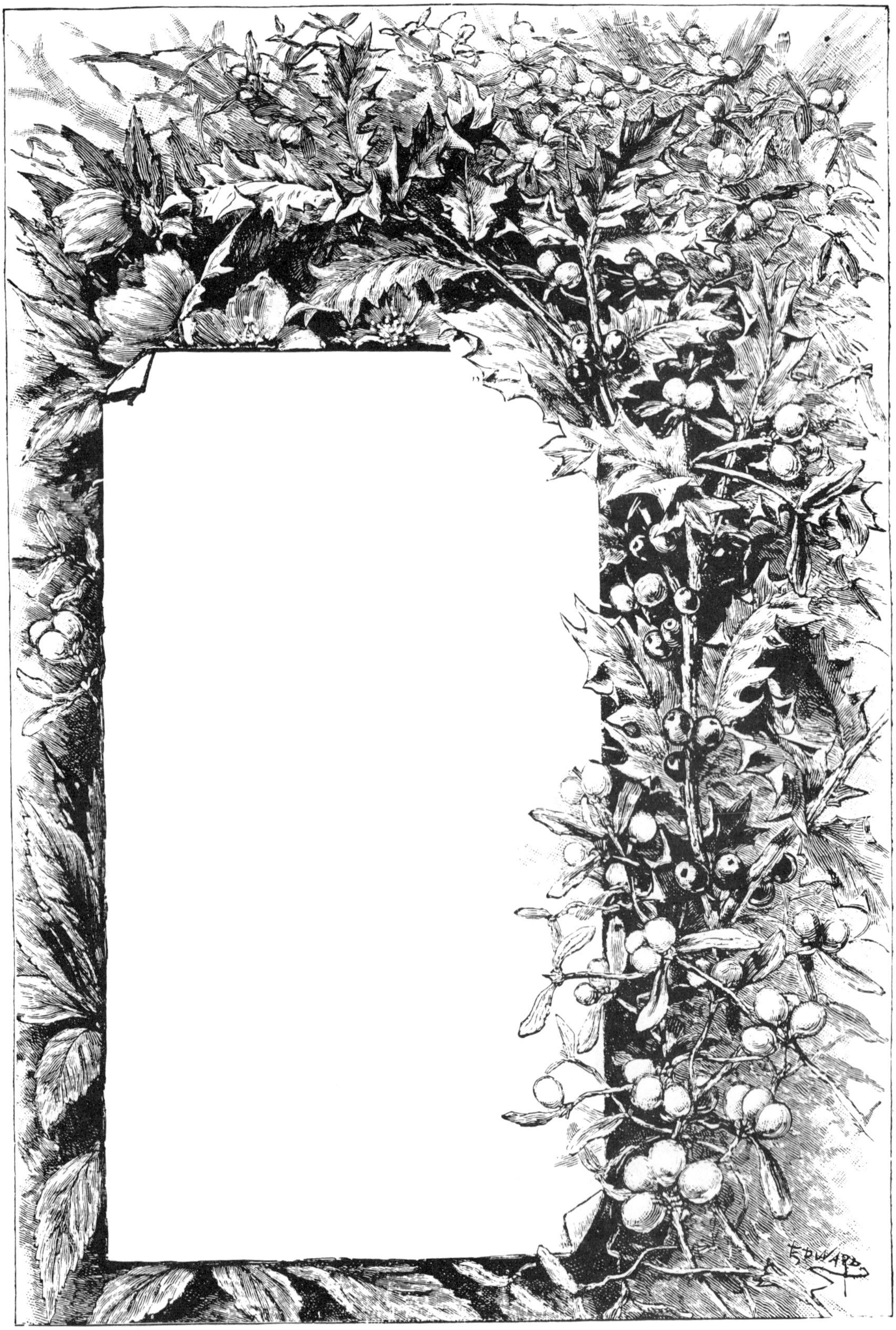

Instant Graphics reproducible page, copyright© 1984

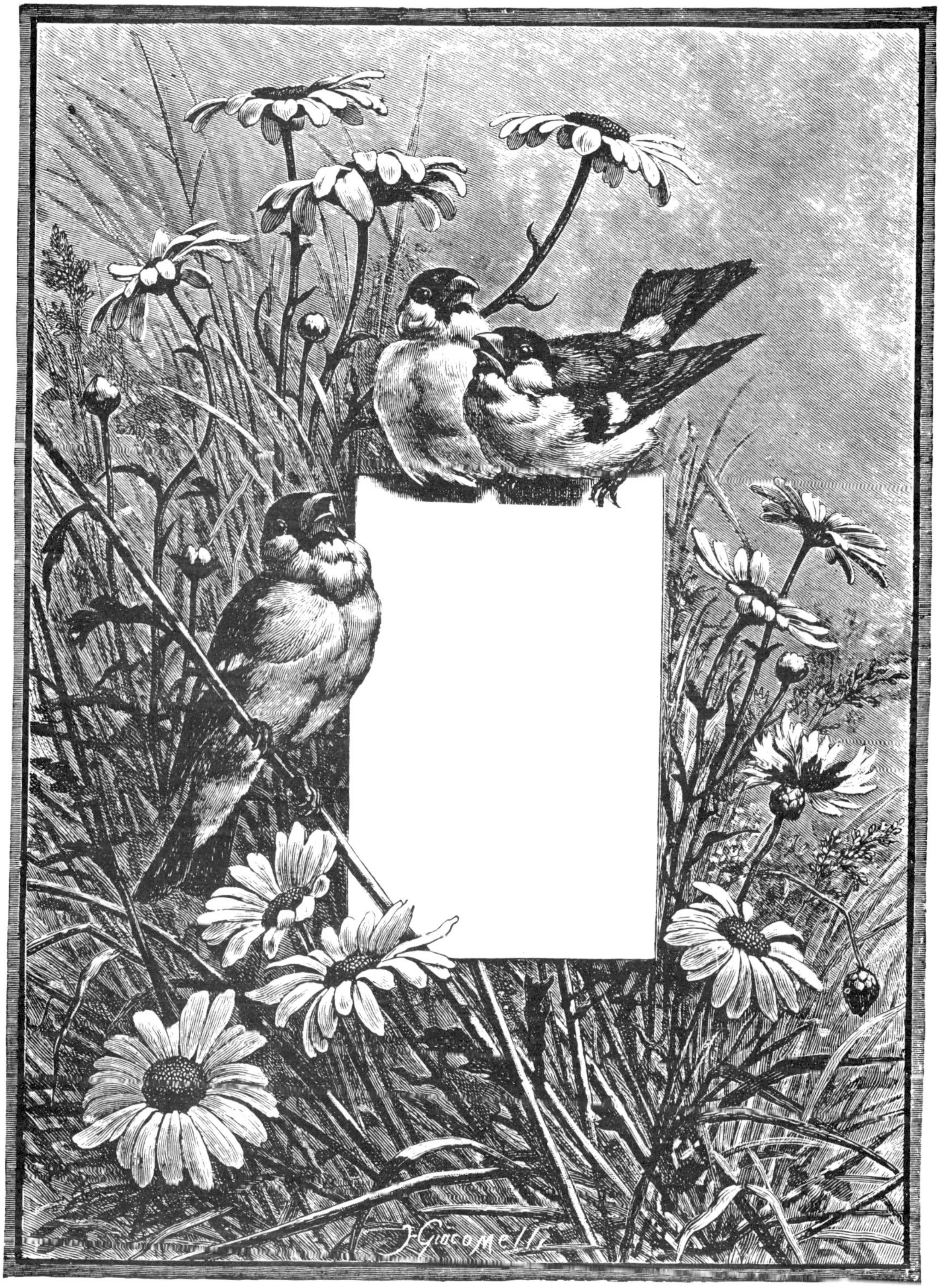

tant Graphics reproducible page, copyright© 1984

Instant Graphics reproducible page, copyright © 1984

83

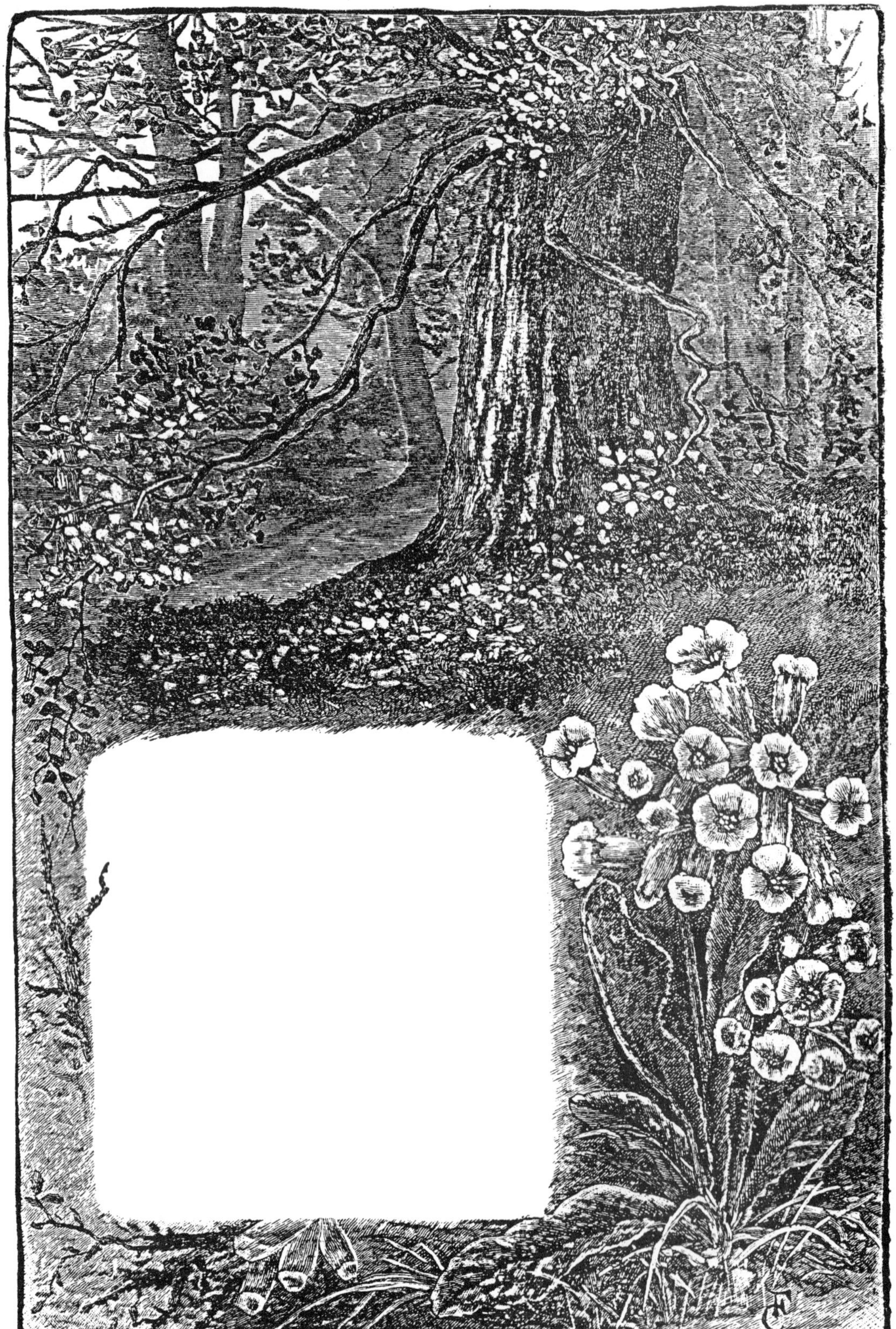

Instant Graphics reproducible page, copyright© 1984

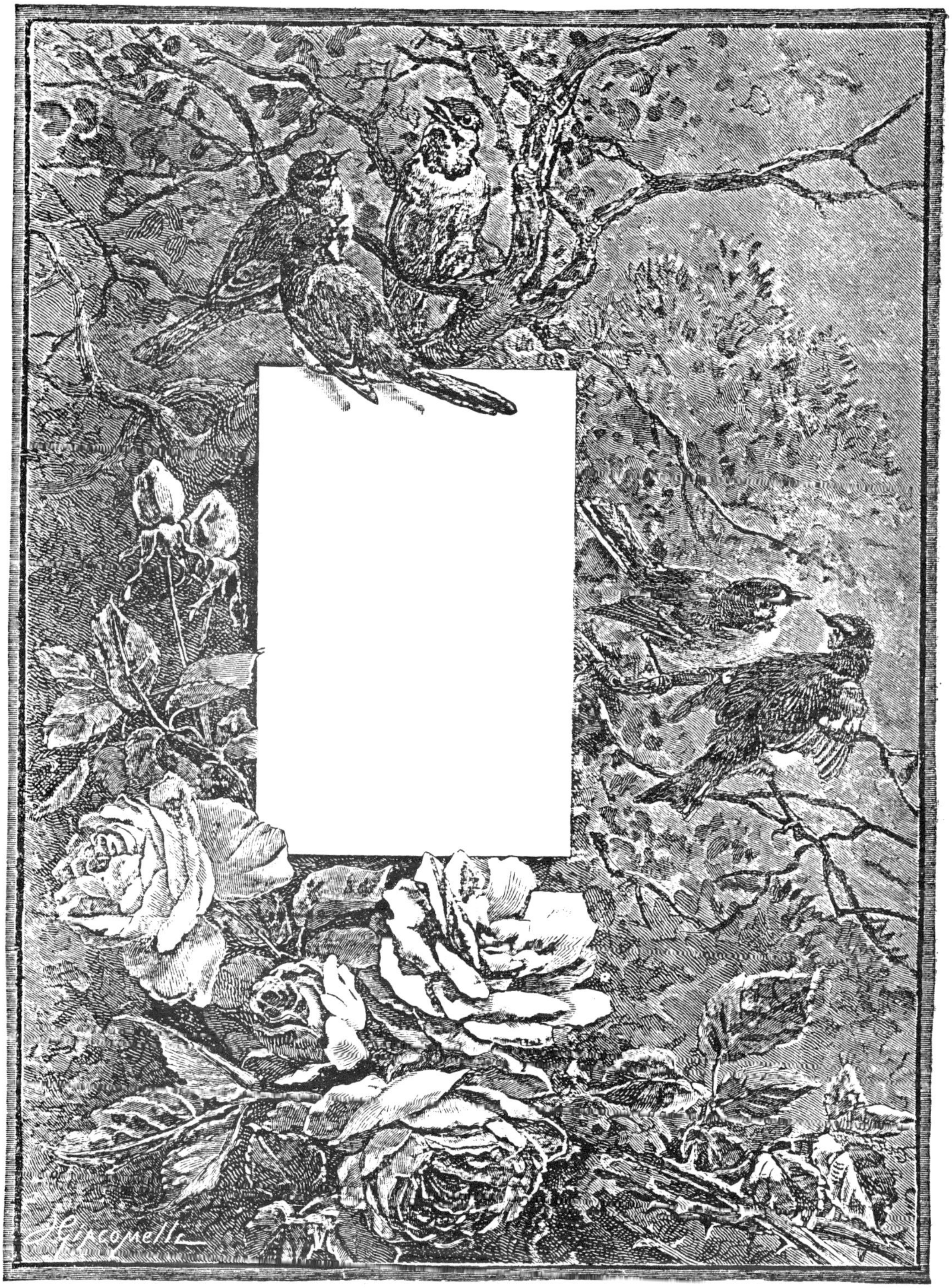

tant Graphics reproducible page, copyright© 1984

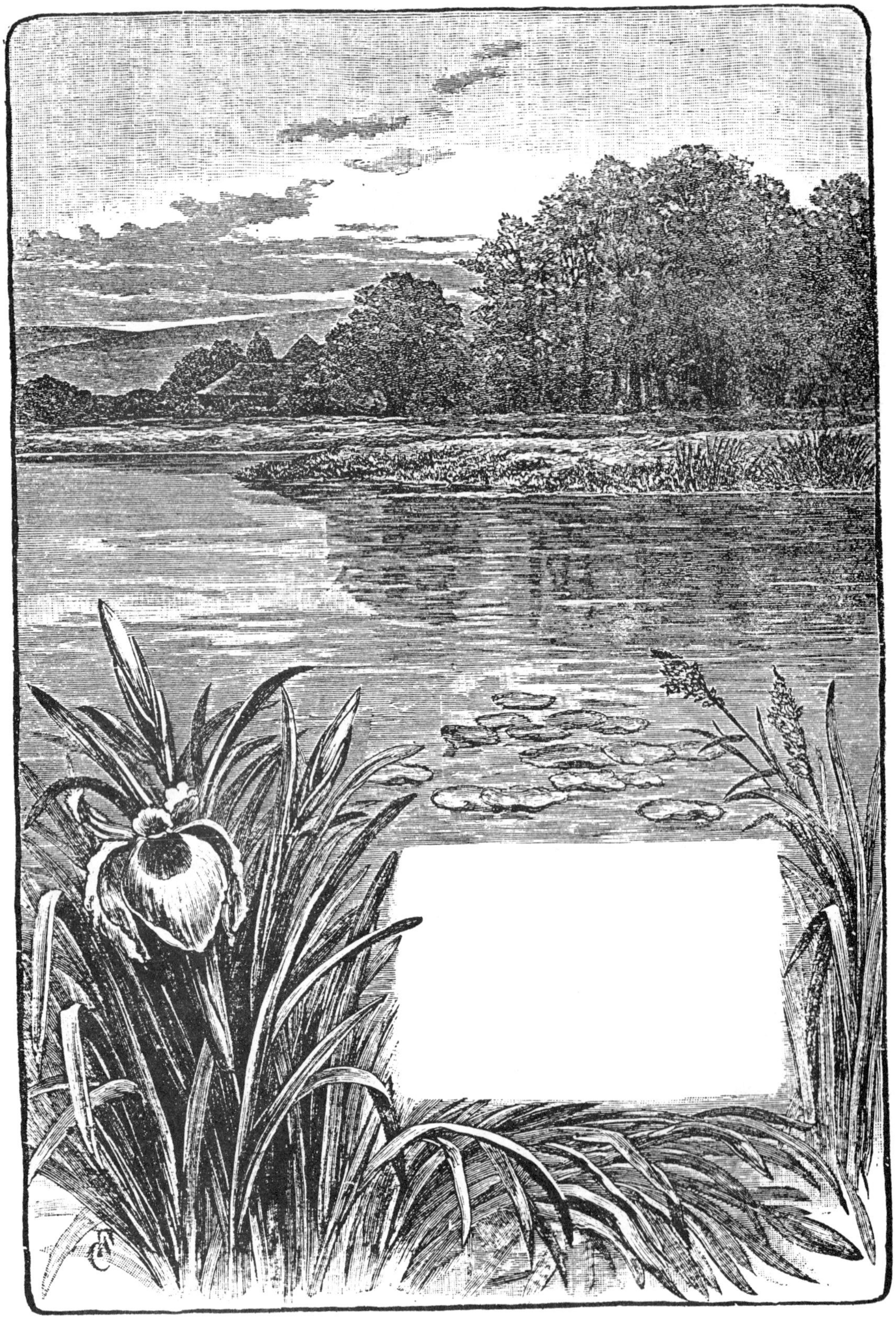

Instant Graphics reproducible page, copyright© 1984

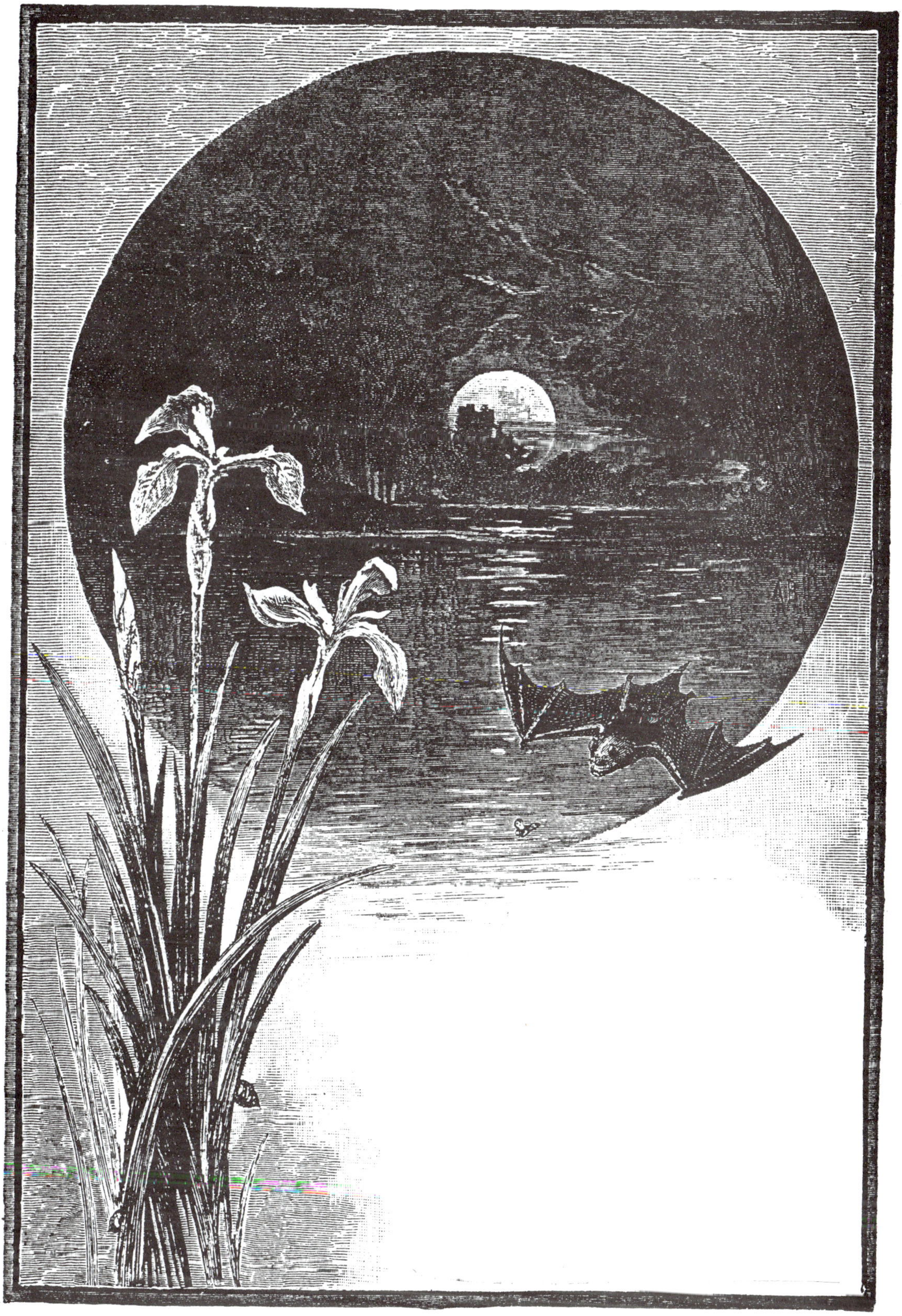

ant Graphics reproducible page, copyright© 1984

Instant Graphics reproducible page, copyright© 1984

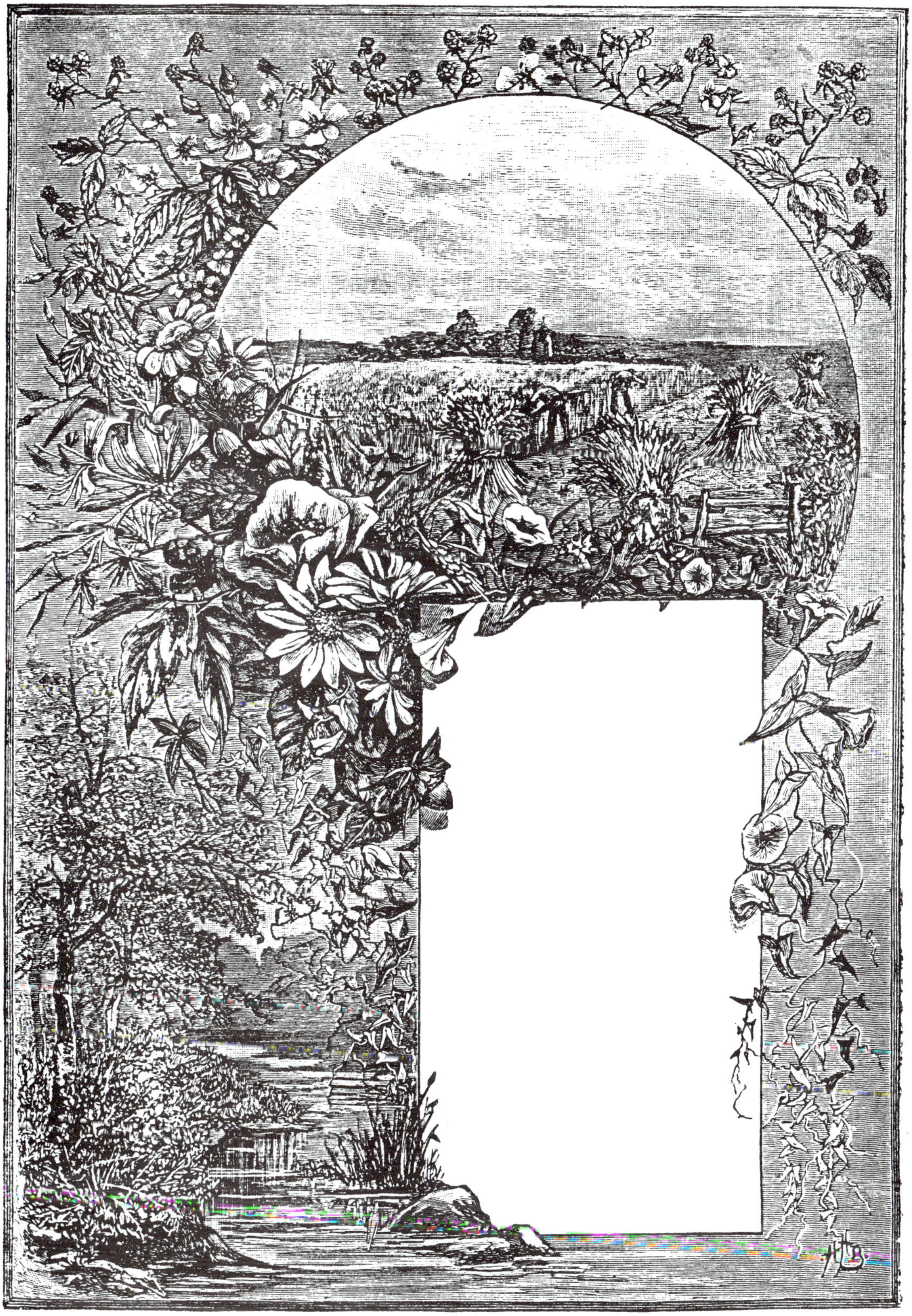

ant Graphics reproducible page, copyright© 1984

Instant Graphics reproducible page, copyright© 1984

91

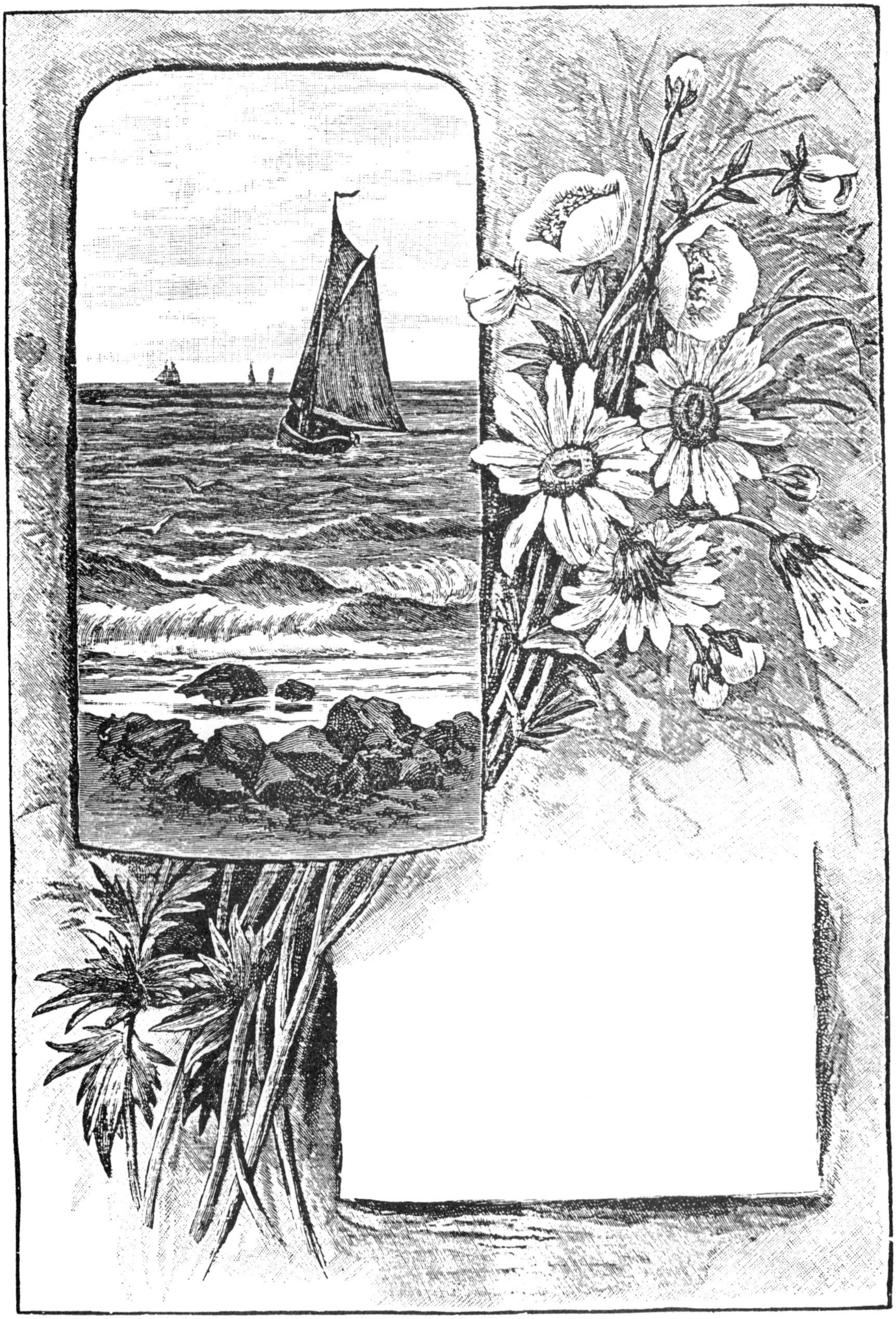

Instant Graphics reproducible page, copyright© 1984

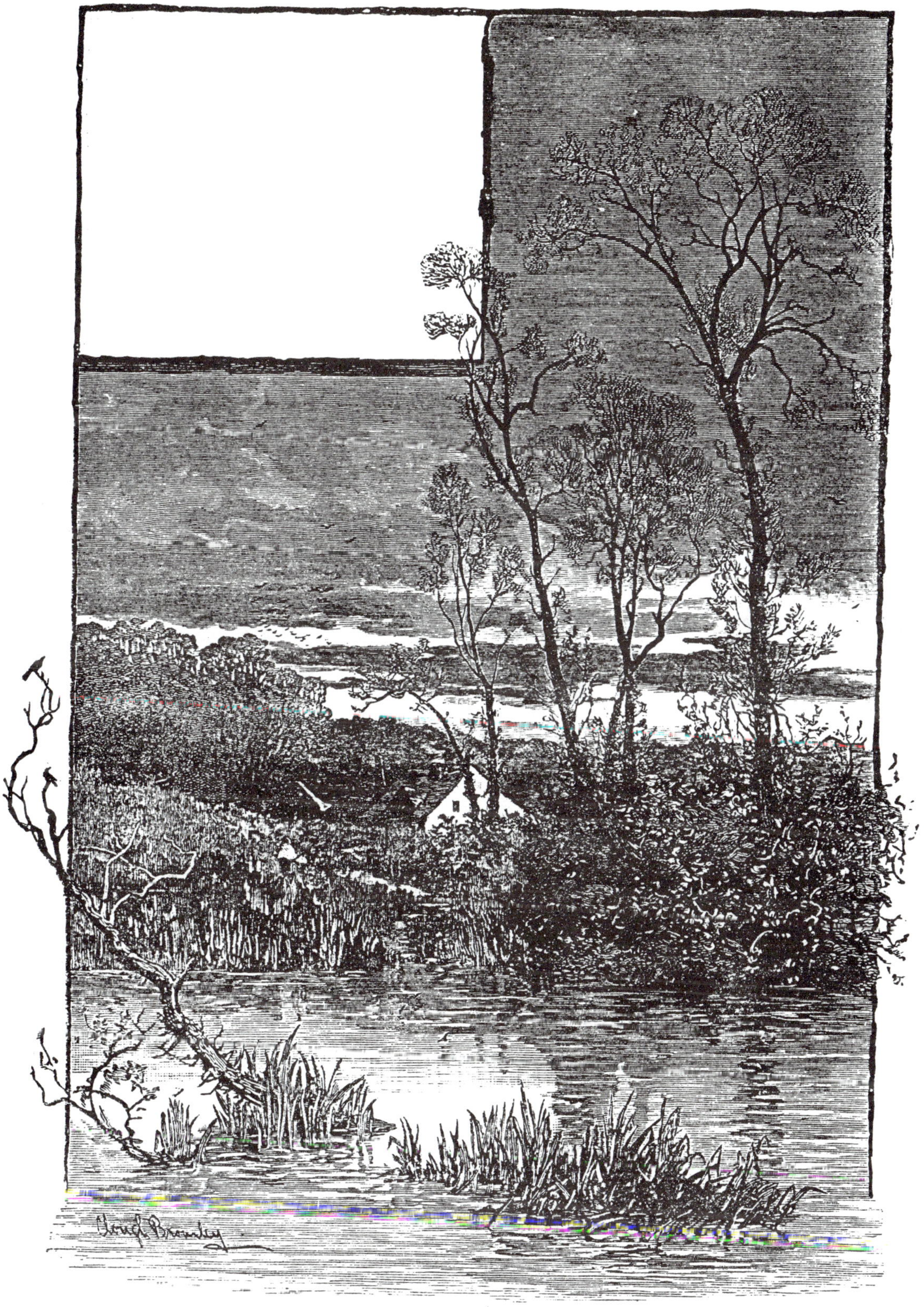

nt Graphics reproducible page, copyright© 1984

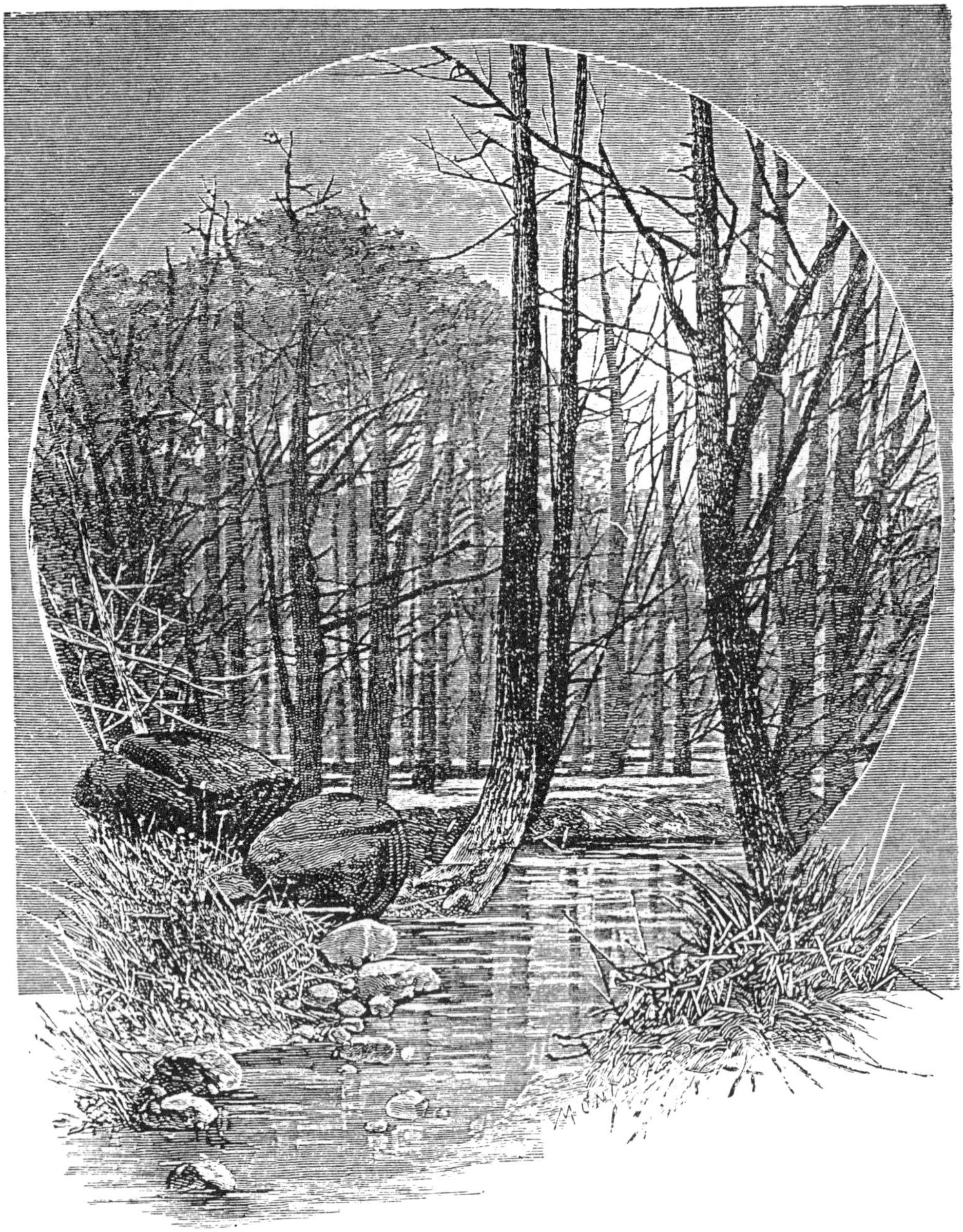

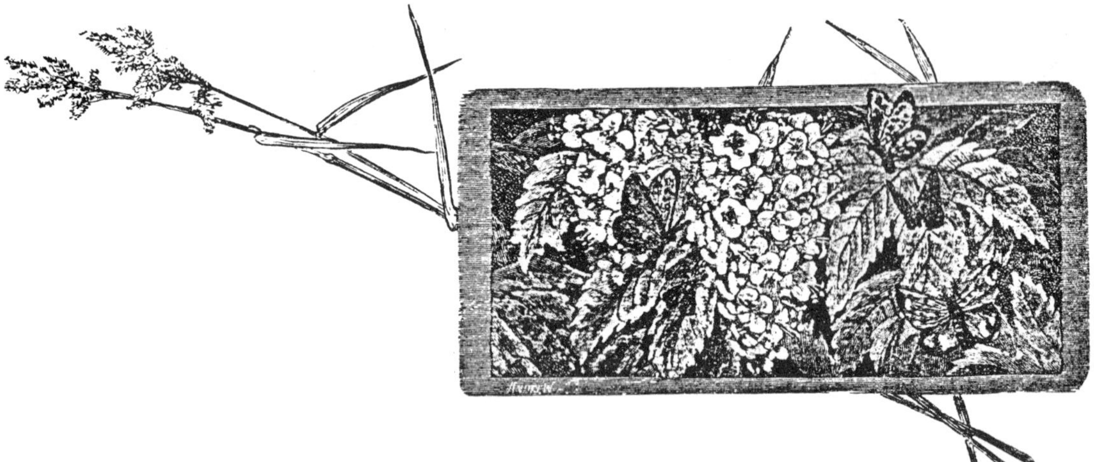

Instant Graphics reproducible page, copyright© 1984

95

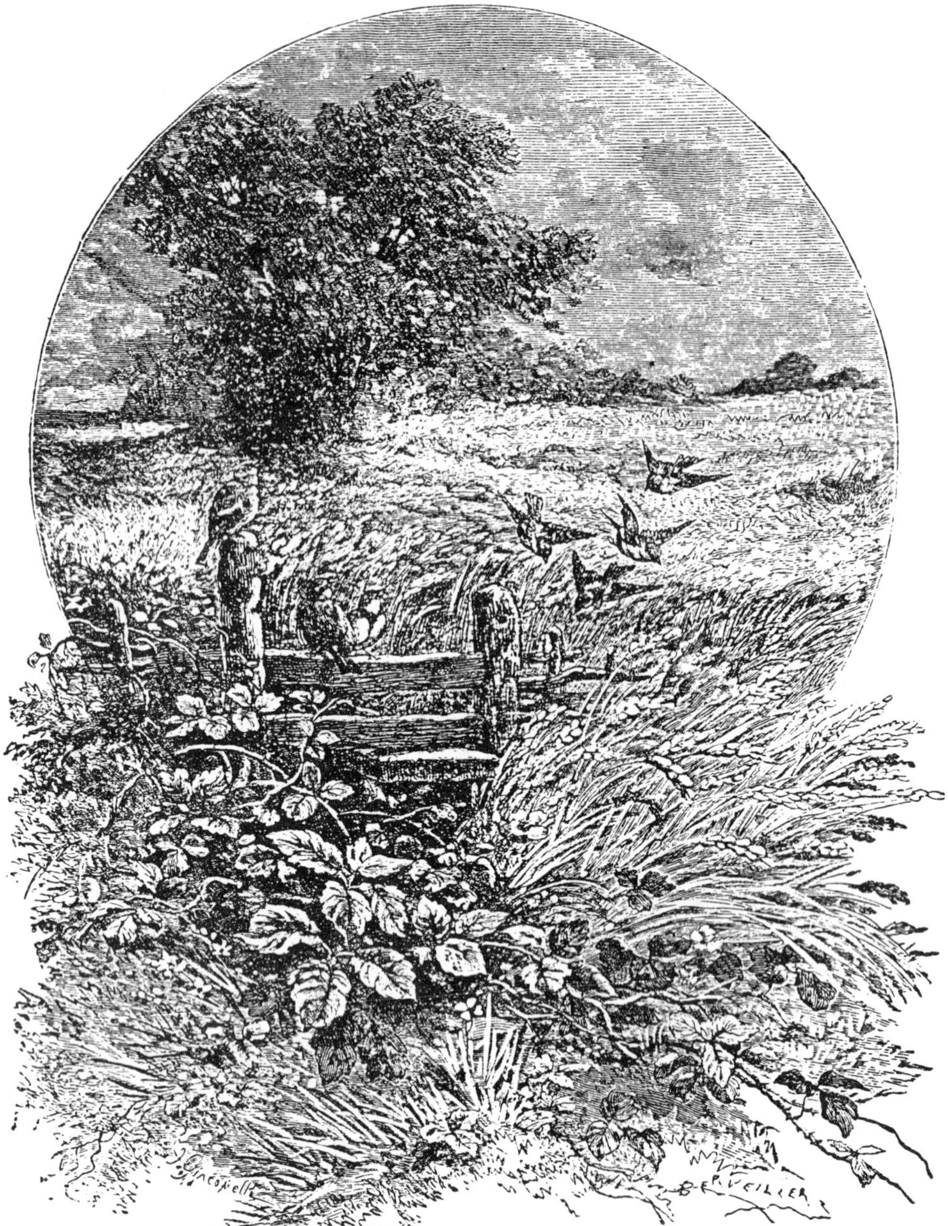

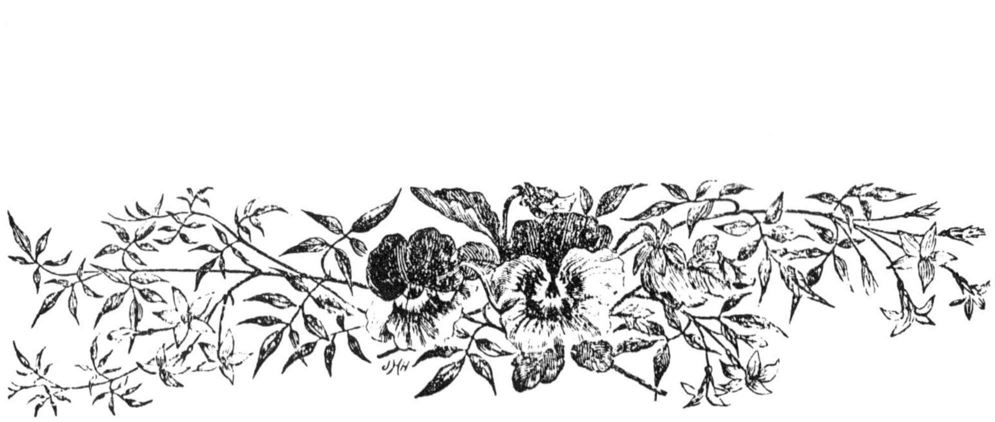

Instant Graphics reproducible page, copyright© 1984

97

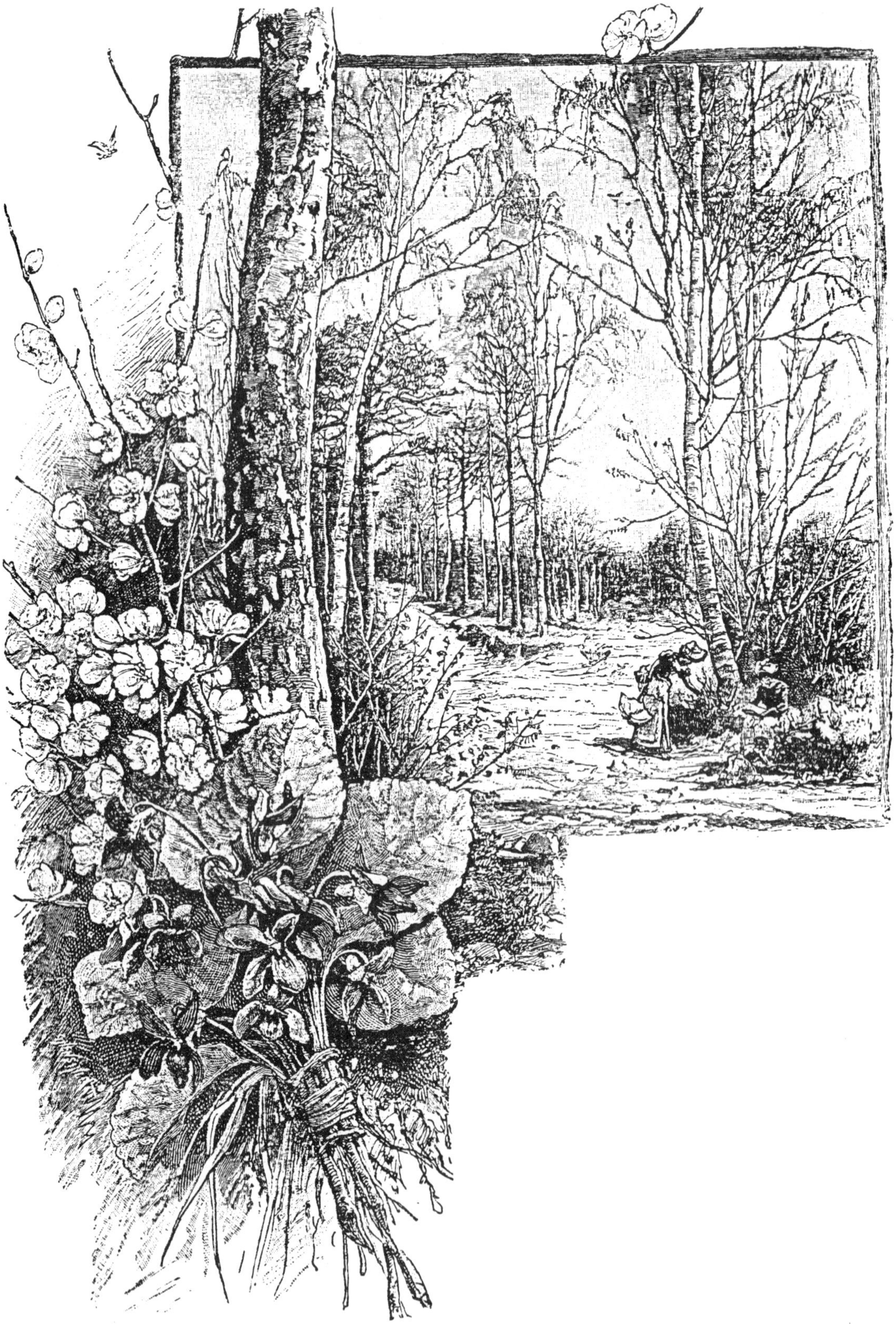

Instant Graphics reproducible page, copyright© 1984

99

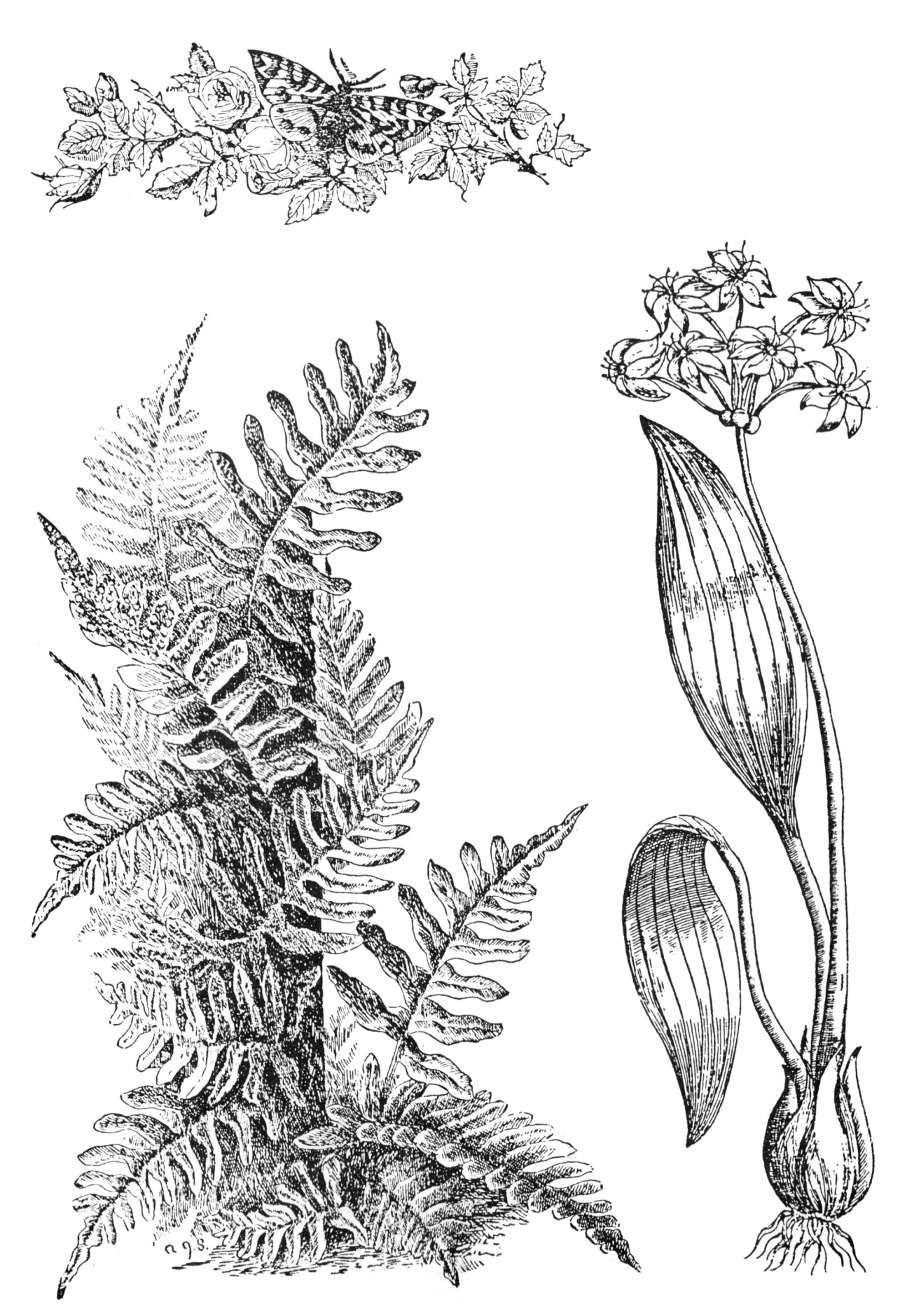

Instant Graphics reproducible page, copyright© 1984

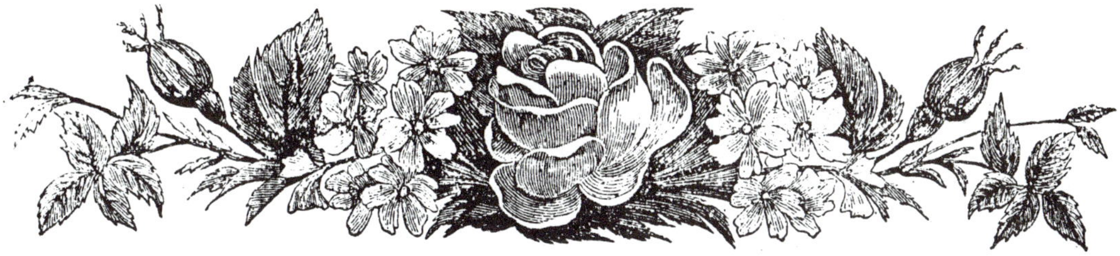

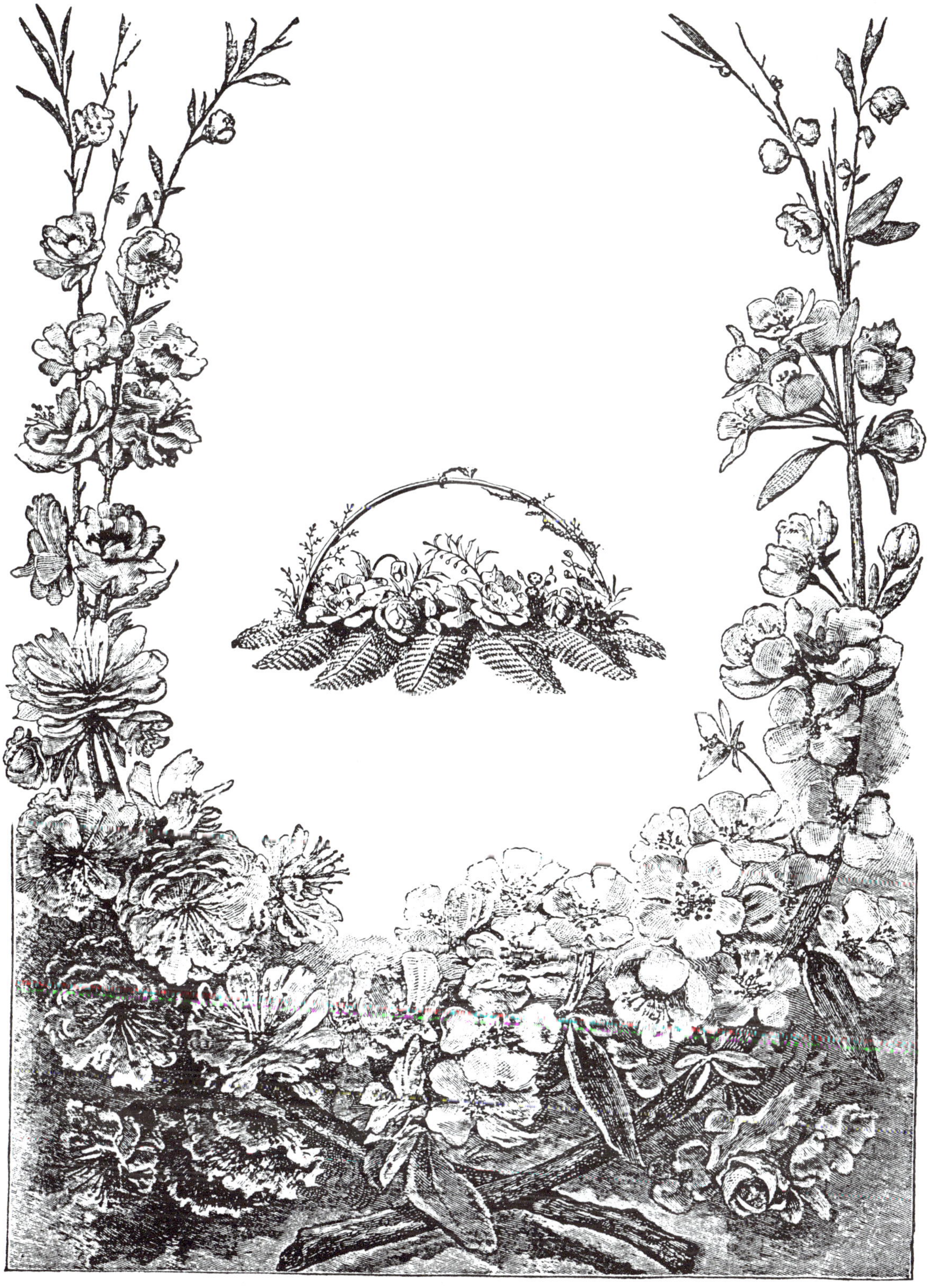

nt Graphics reproducible page, copyright© 1984

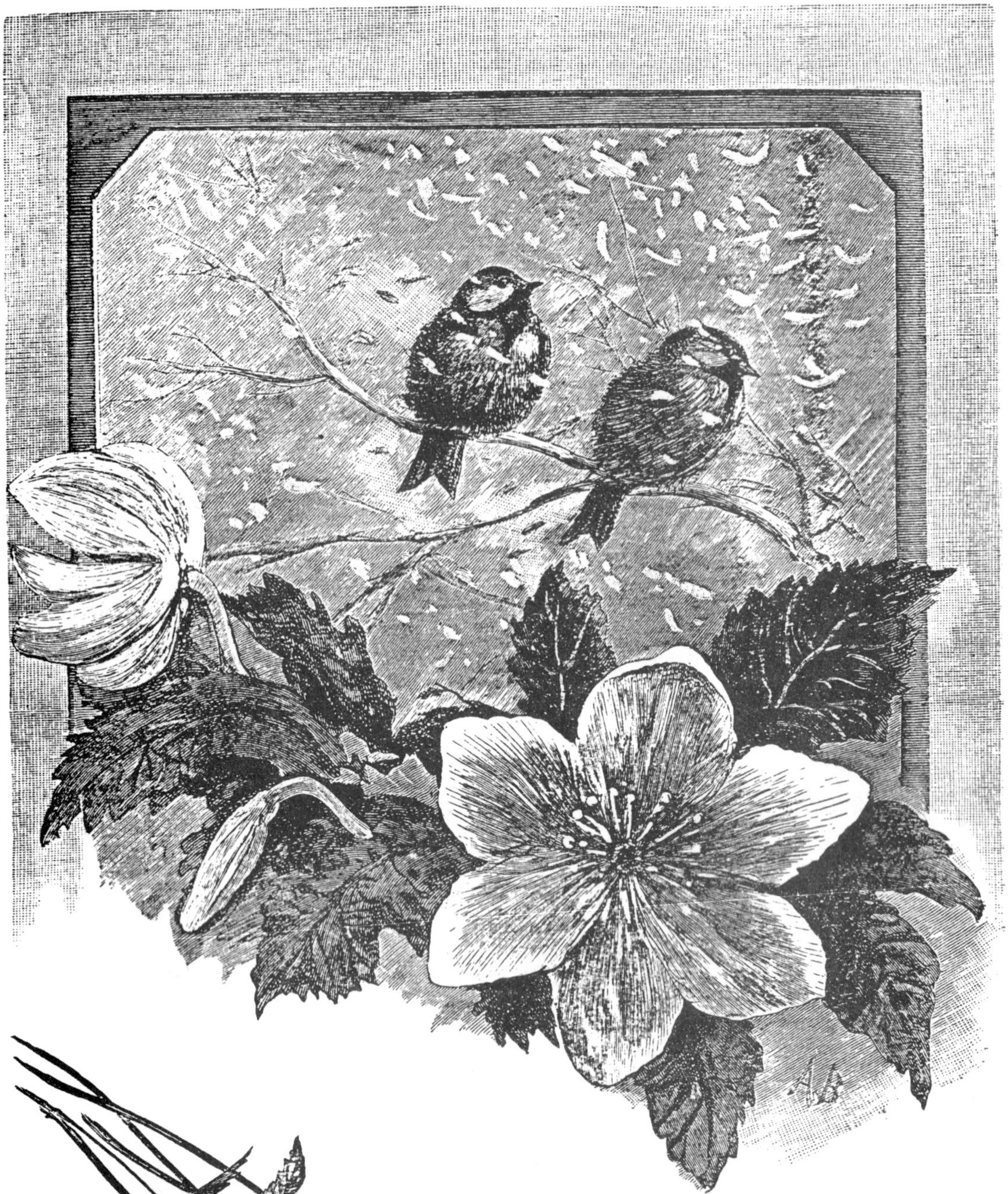

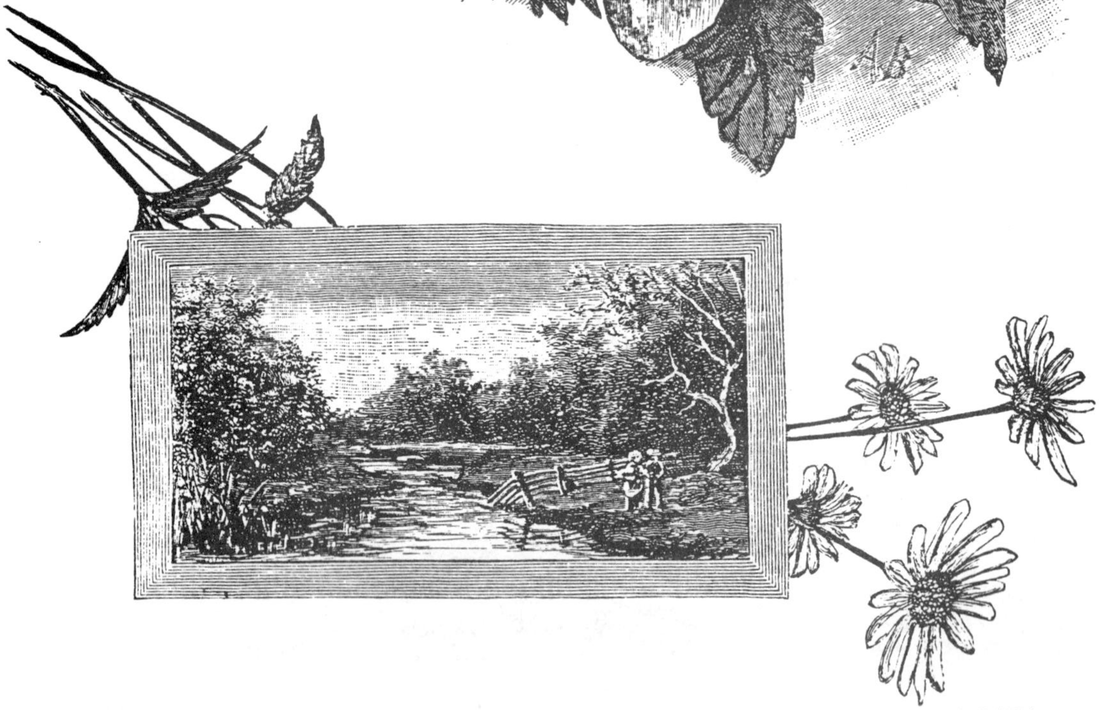

Instant Graphics reproducible page, copyright© 1984

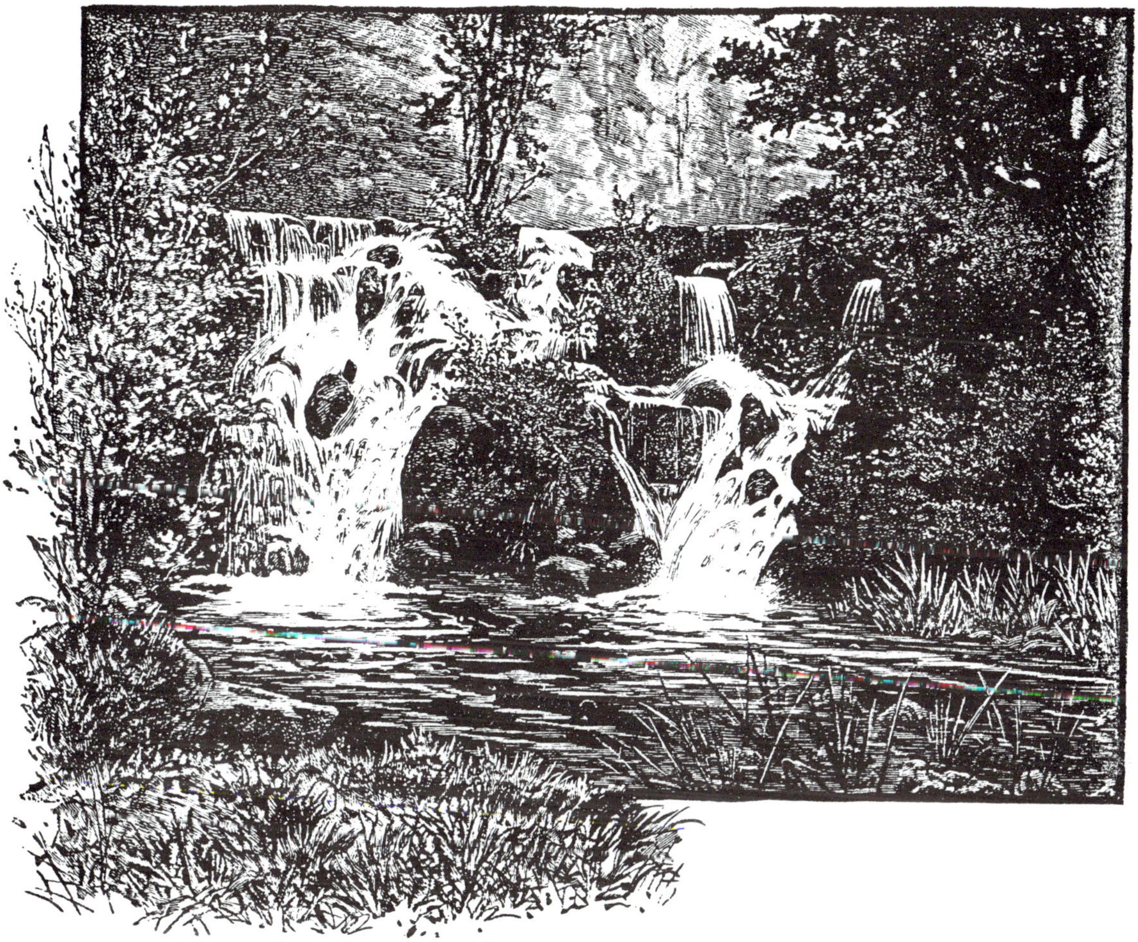

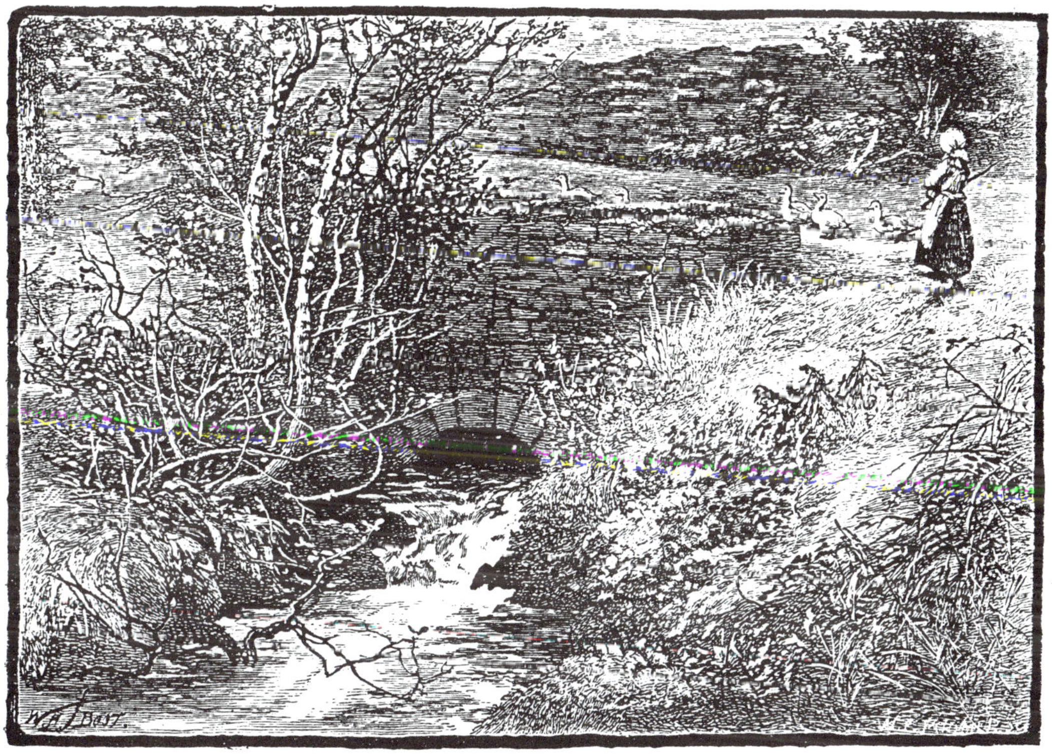

ant Graphics reproducible page, copyright© 1984

Instant Graphics reproducible page, copyright© 1984

105

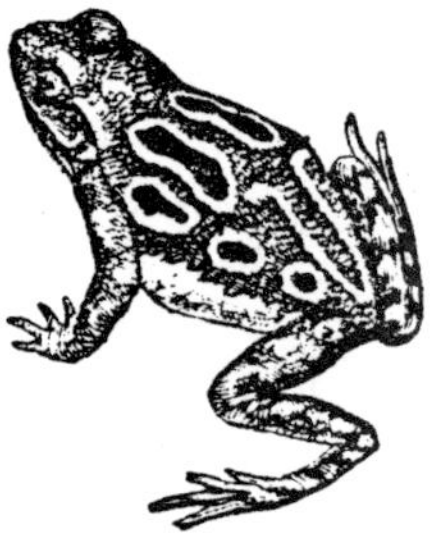

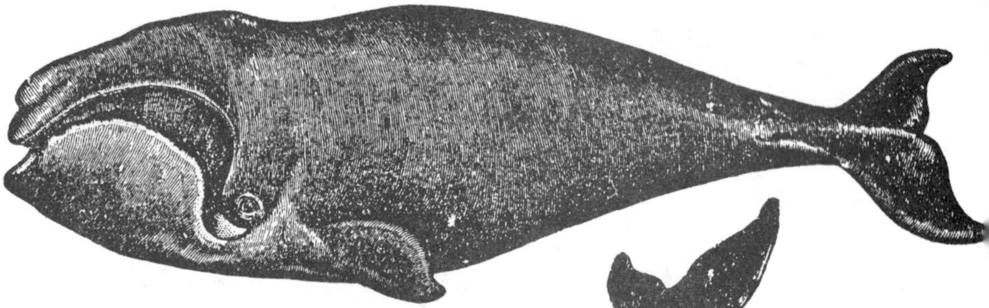

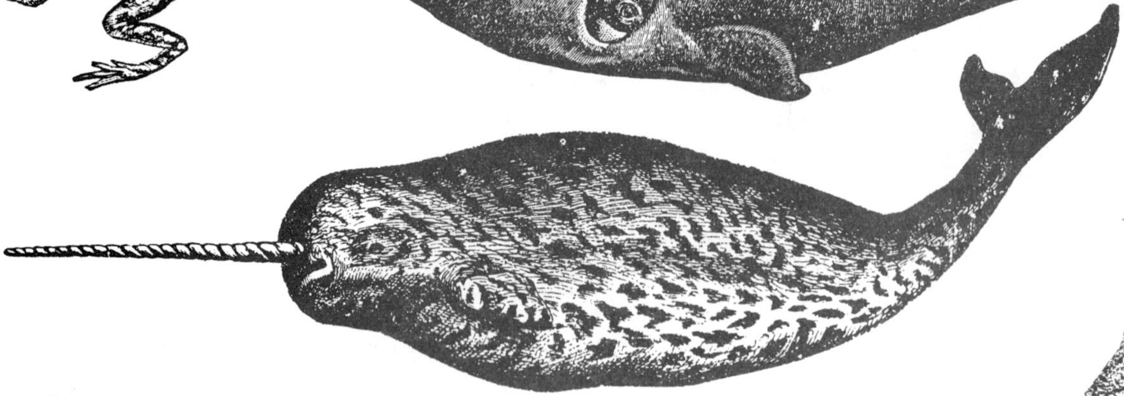

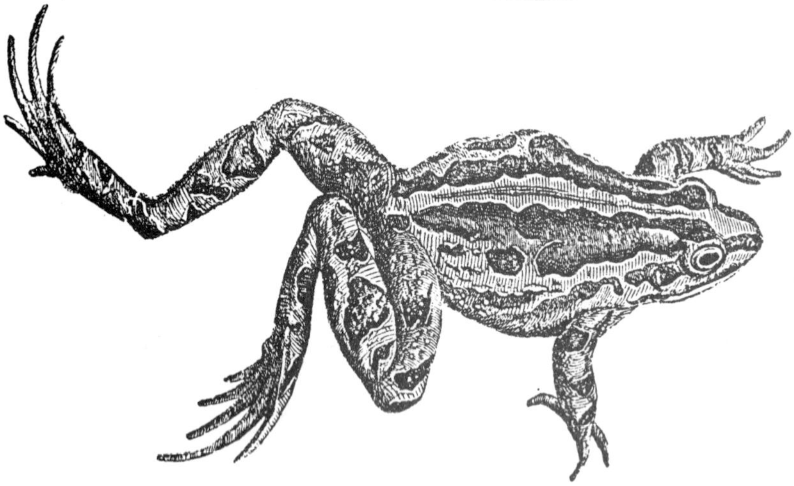

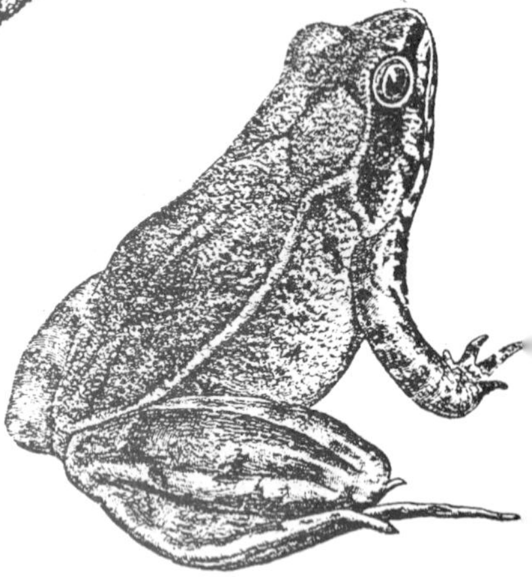

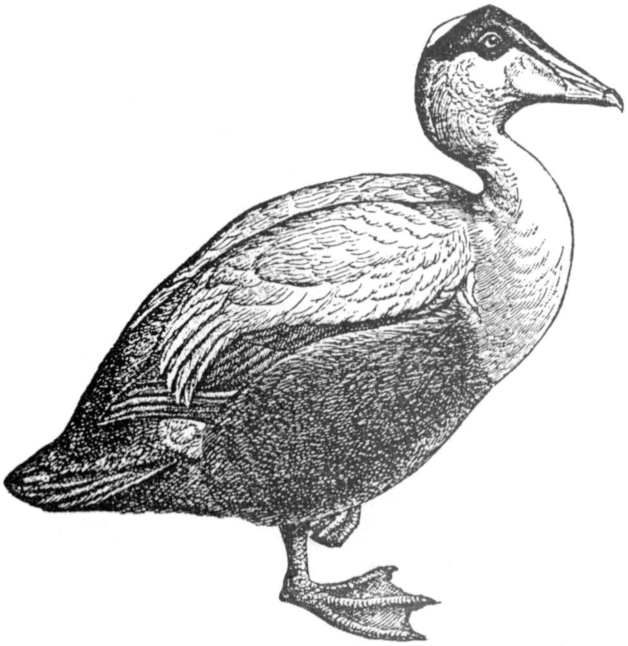

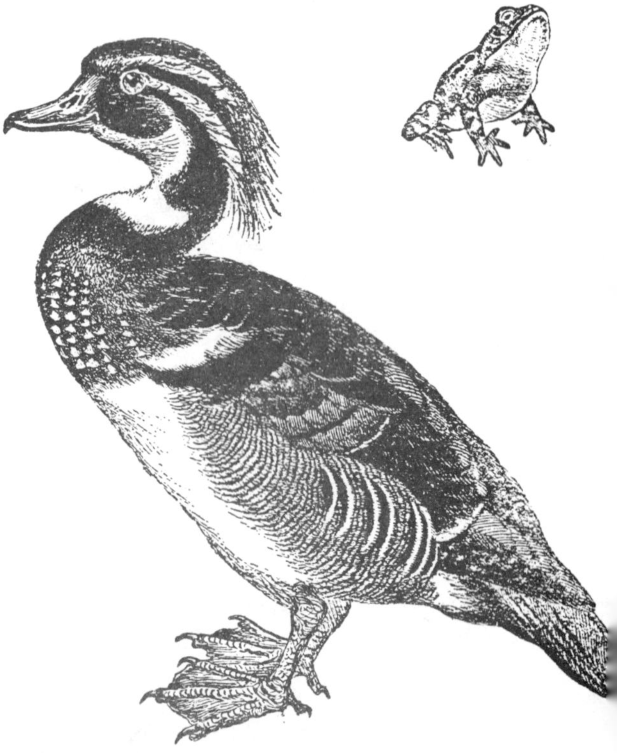

Instant Graphics reproducible page, copyright© 1984

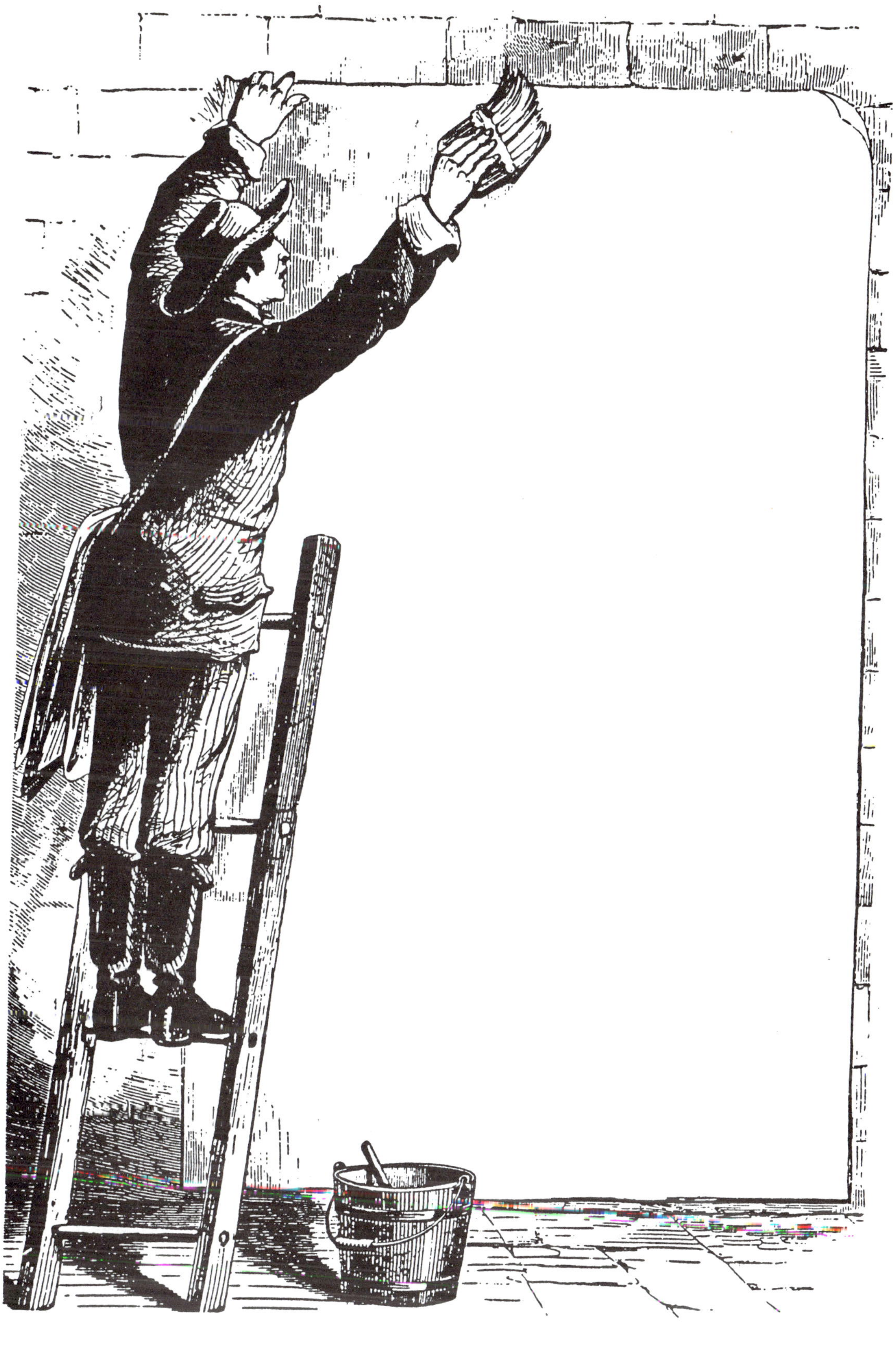

ınt Graphics reproducible page, copyright© 1984

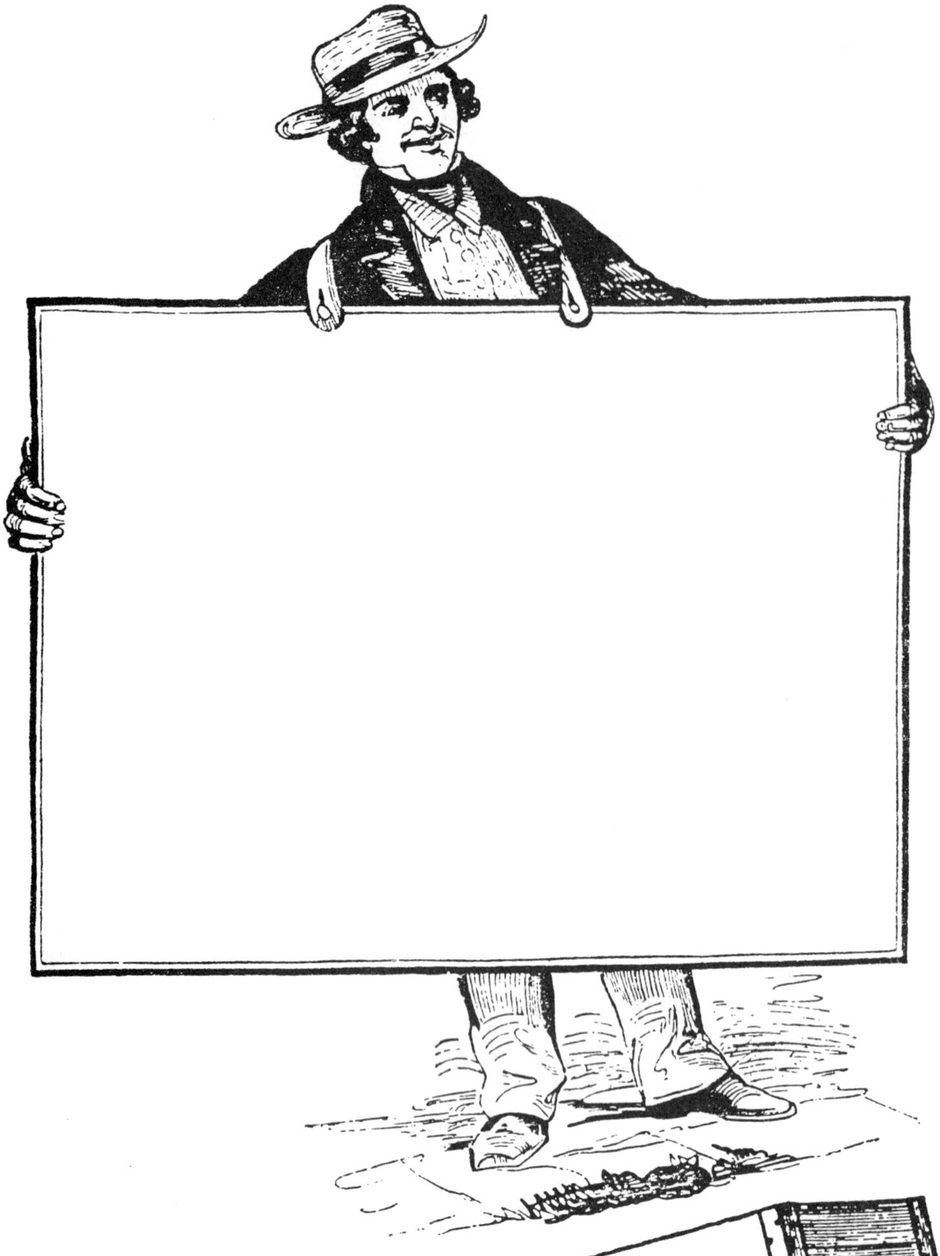

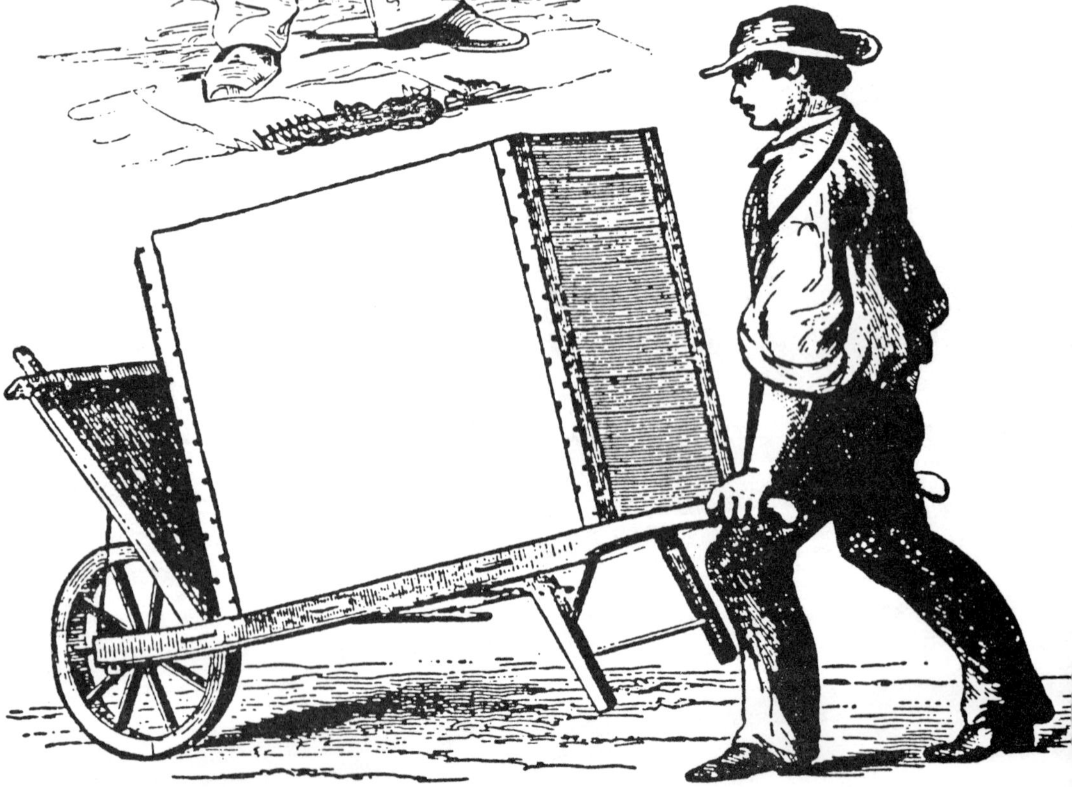

Instant Graphics reproducible page, copyright© 1984

CHRISTMAS POEMS & PICTURES

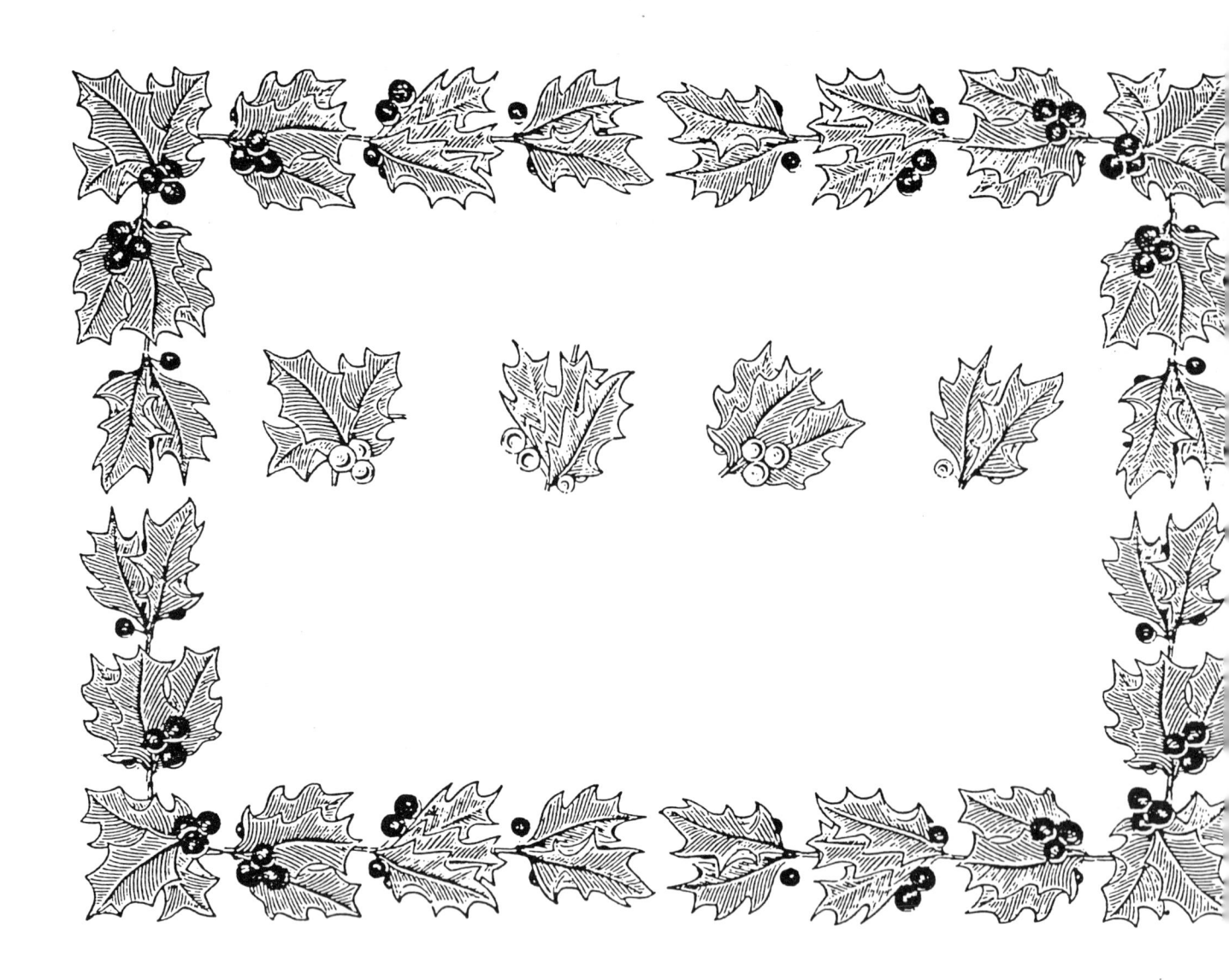

Instant Graphics reproducible page, copyright © 1984

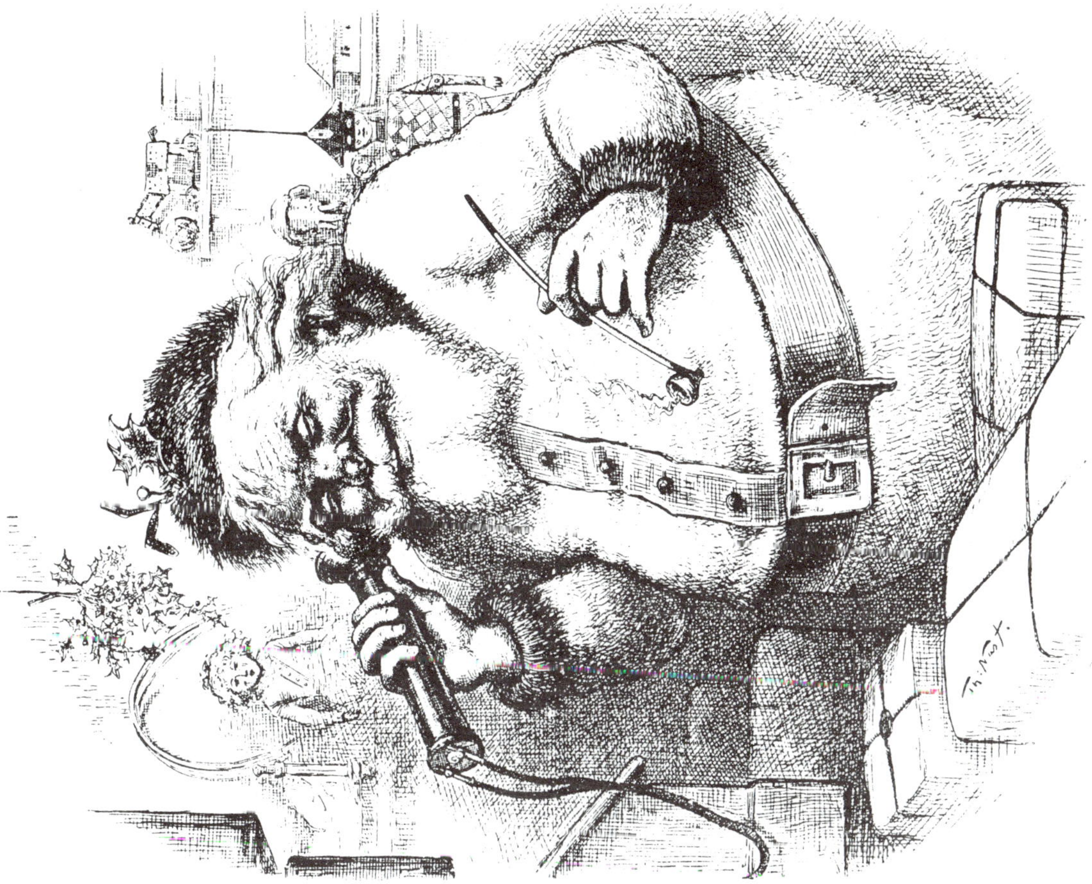

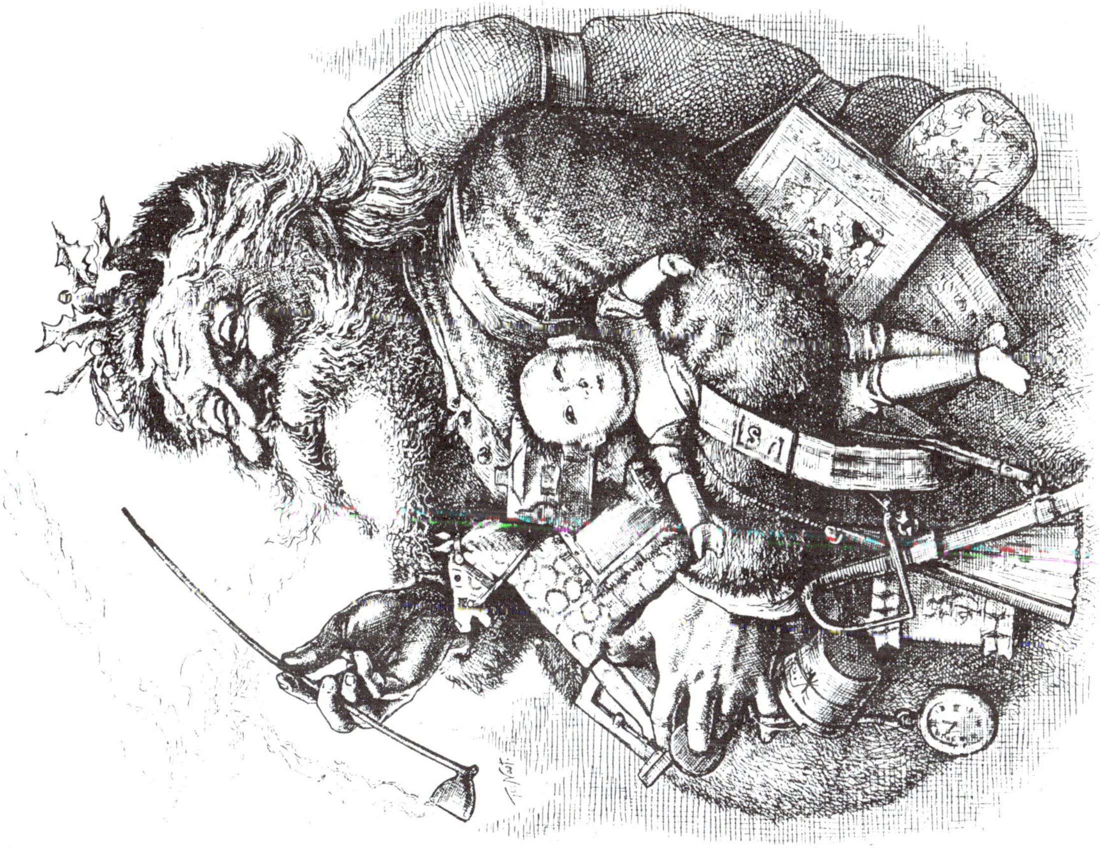

ant Graphics reproducible page, copyright© 1984

ABCDE
FGHIJ
KLMNO
PQRST
UVWX
YZ&

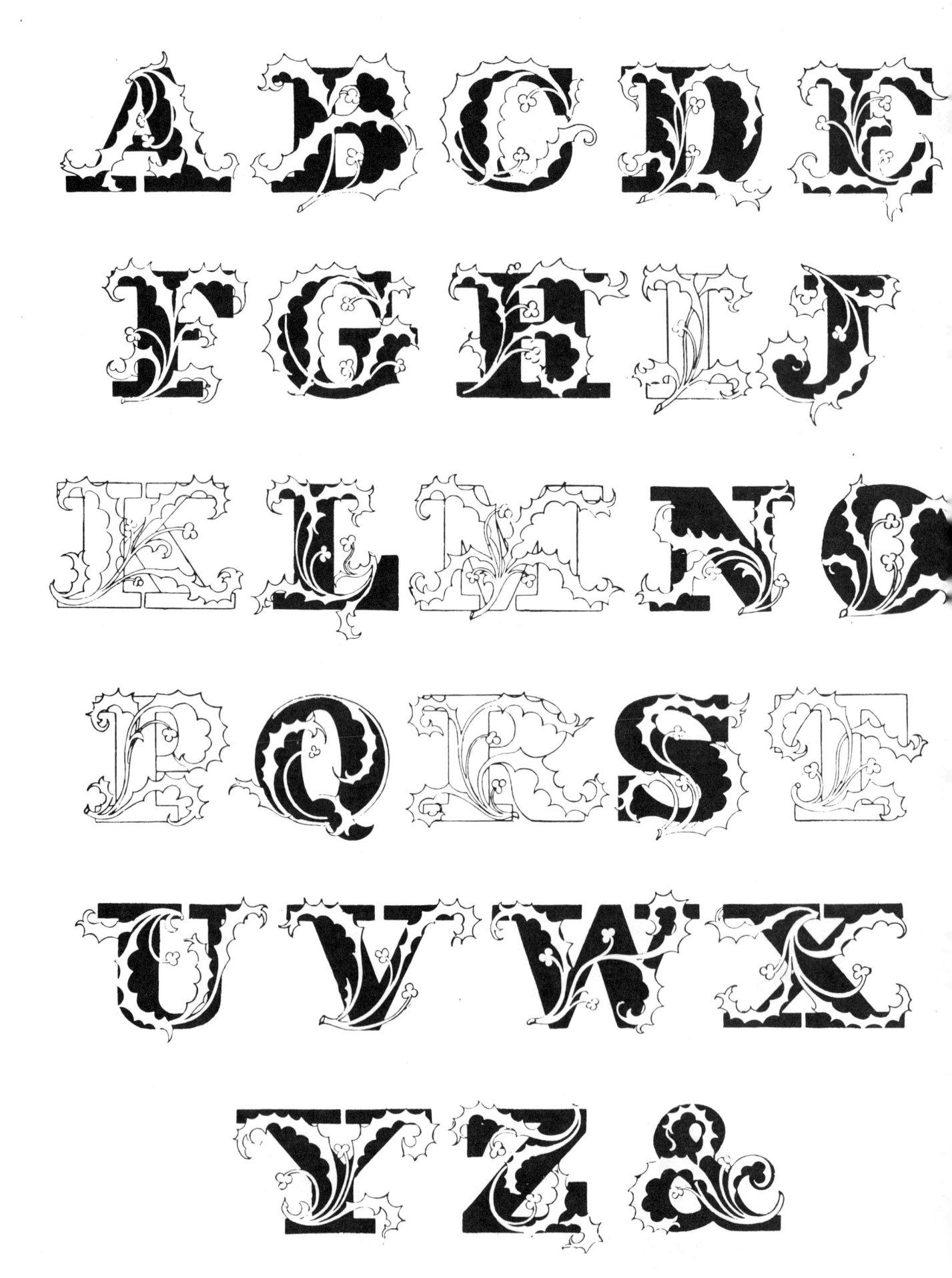

Instant Graphics reproducible page, copyright© 1984

113

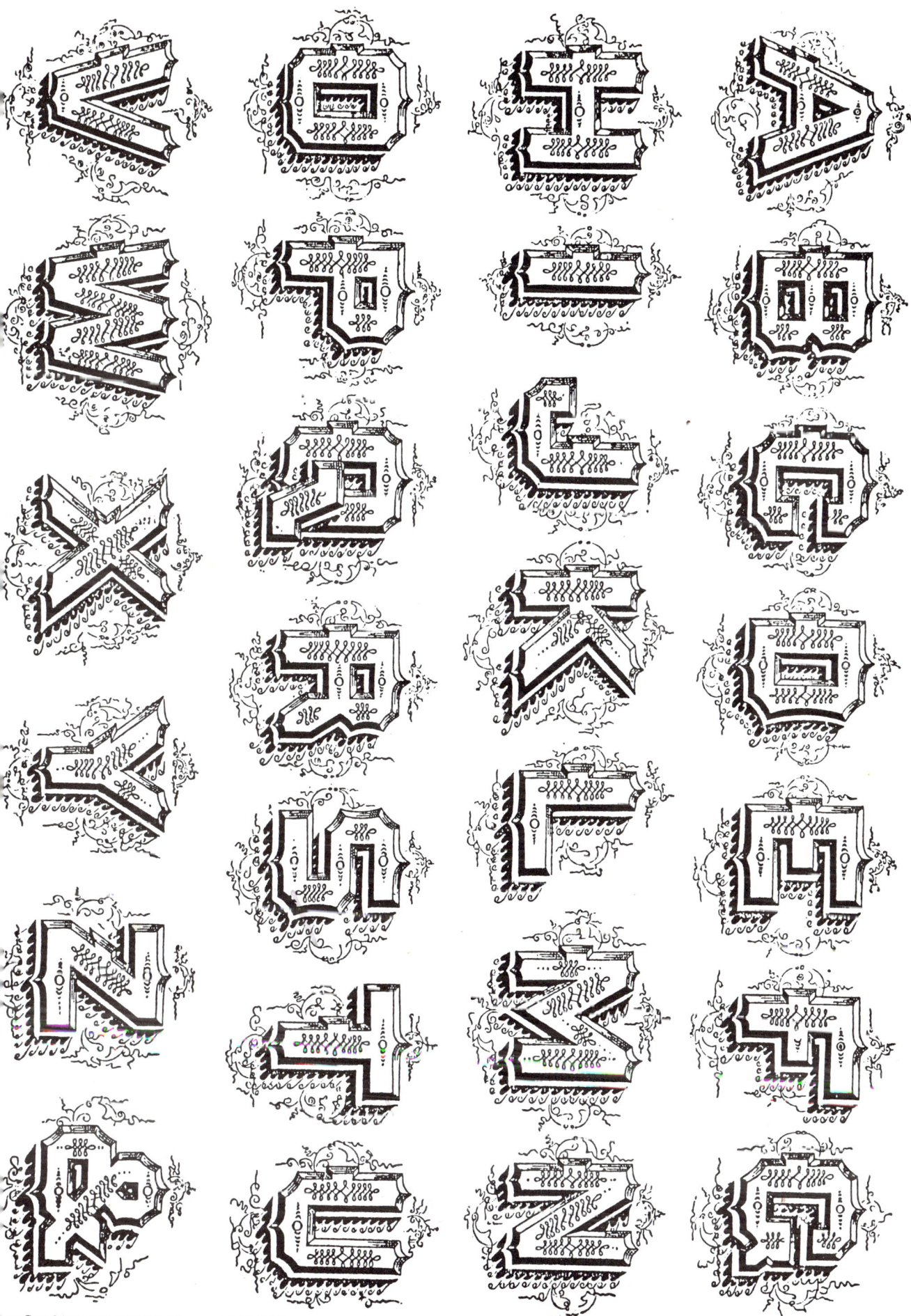

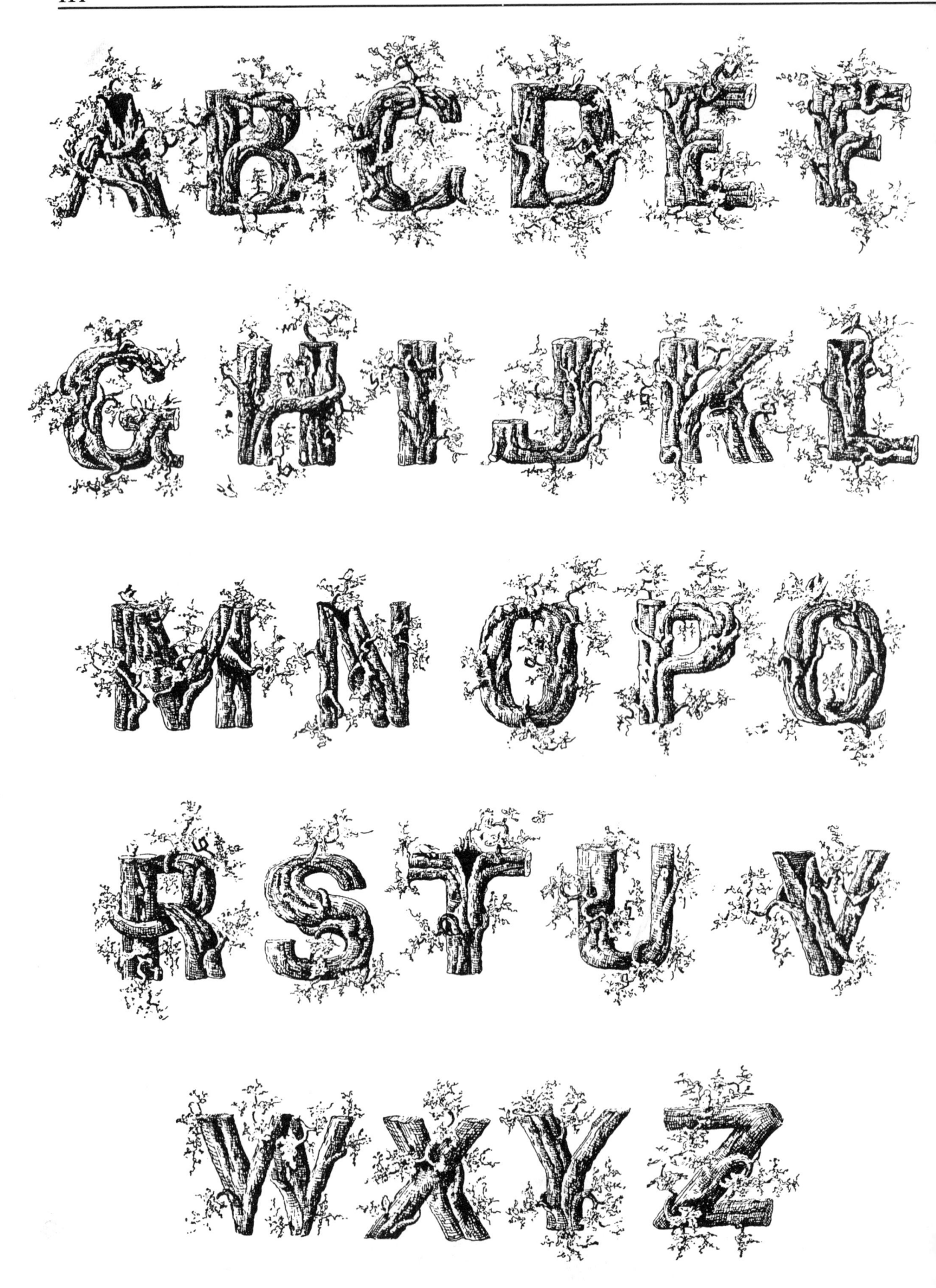

ABCDEF
GHIJKL
MNOPQ
RSTUV
WXYZ

Instant Graphics reproducible page, copyright© 1984

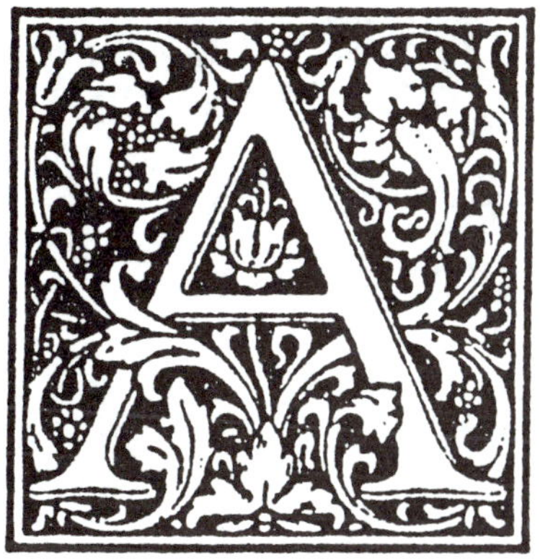

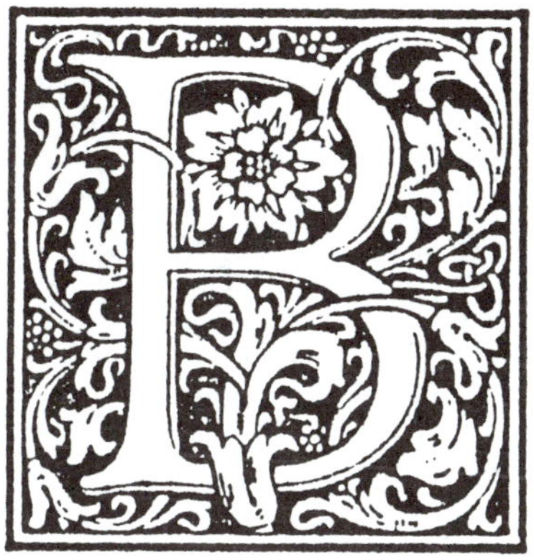

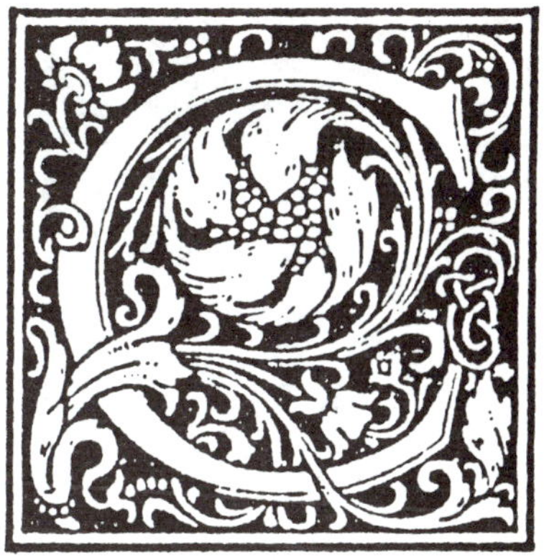

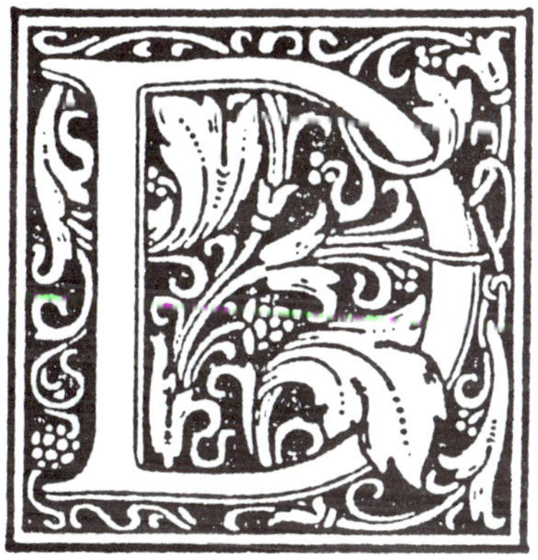

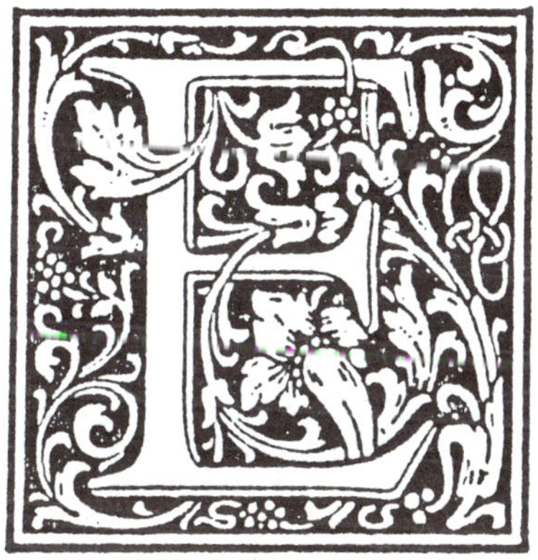

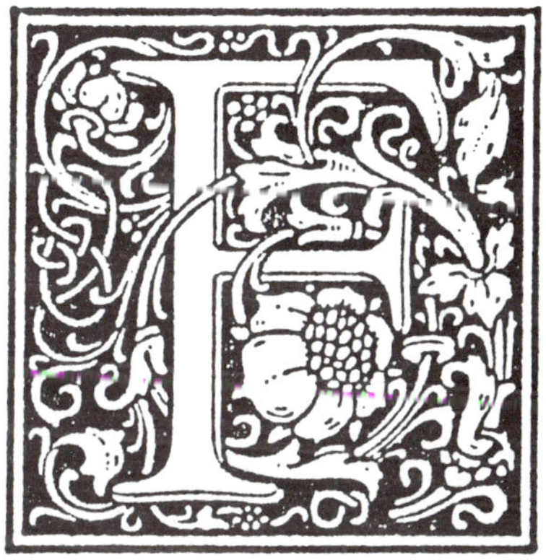

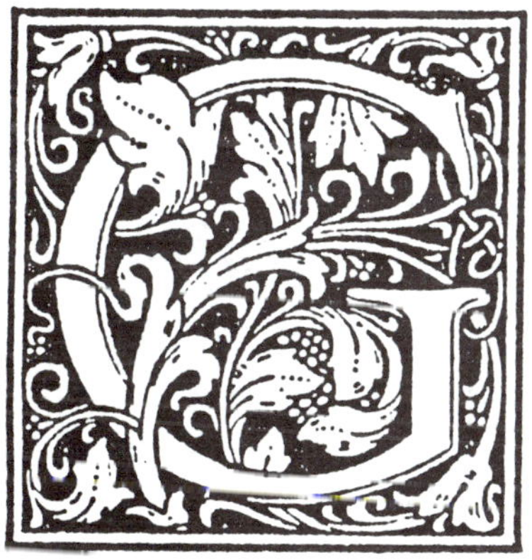

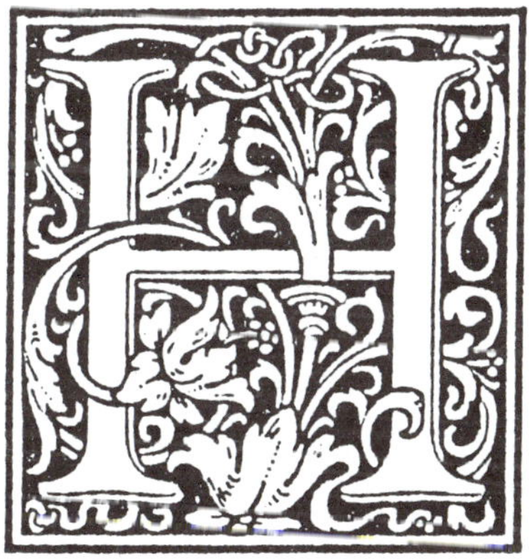

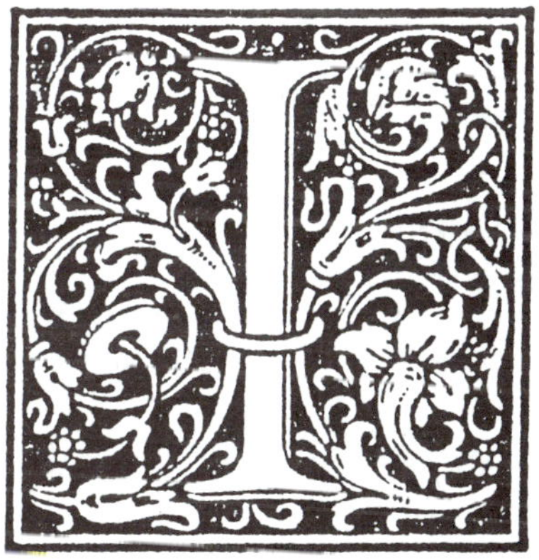

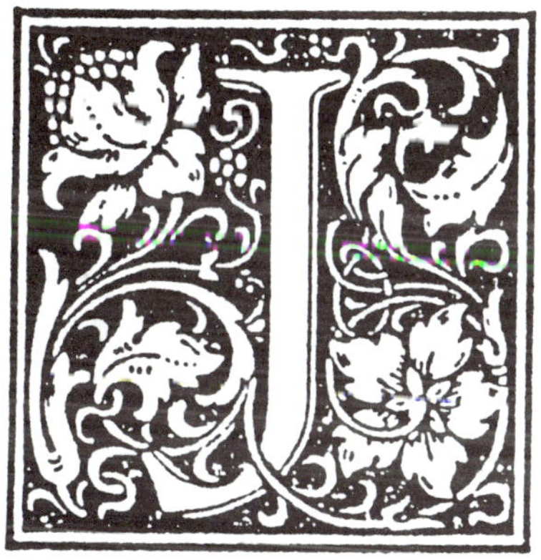

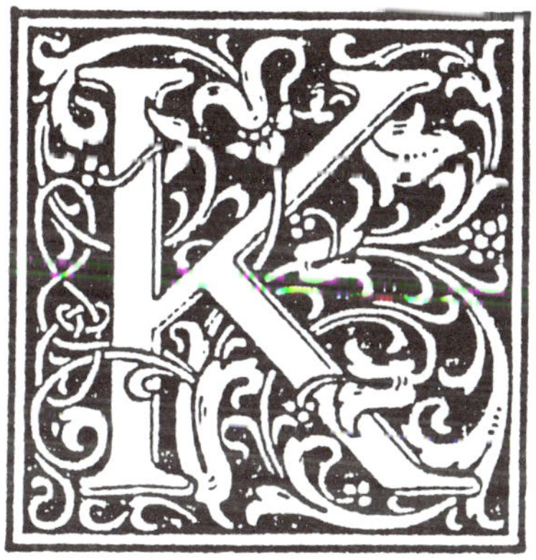

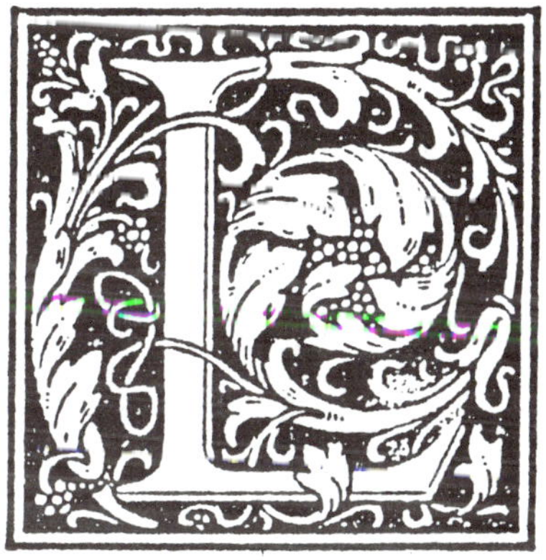

ant Graphics reproducible page, copyright© 1984

Instant Graphics reproducible page, copyright© 1984

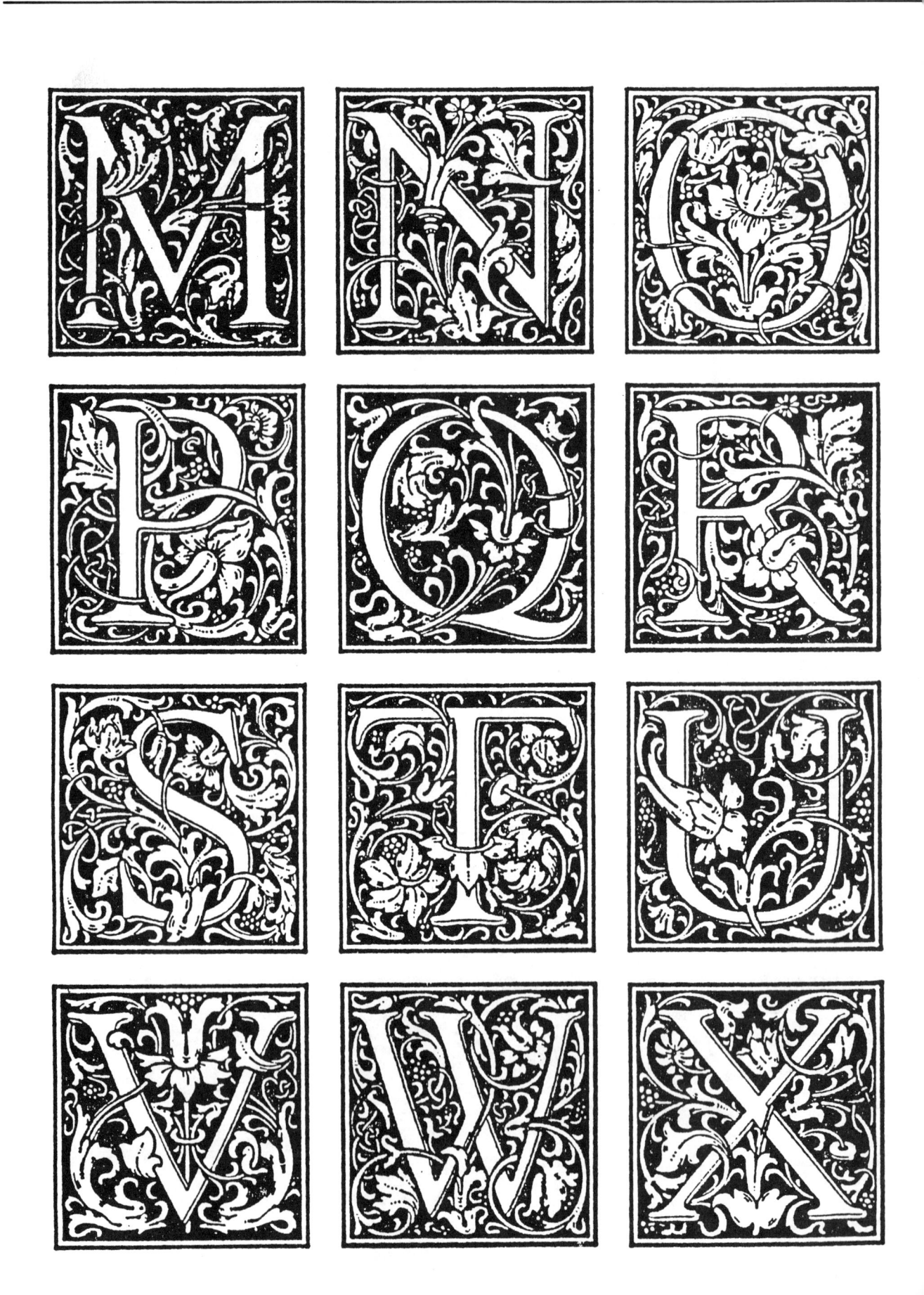

ABCDE
FGHIJ
KLMNO
PQRST
UVWX
YZ

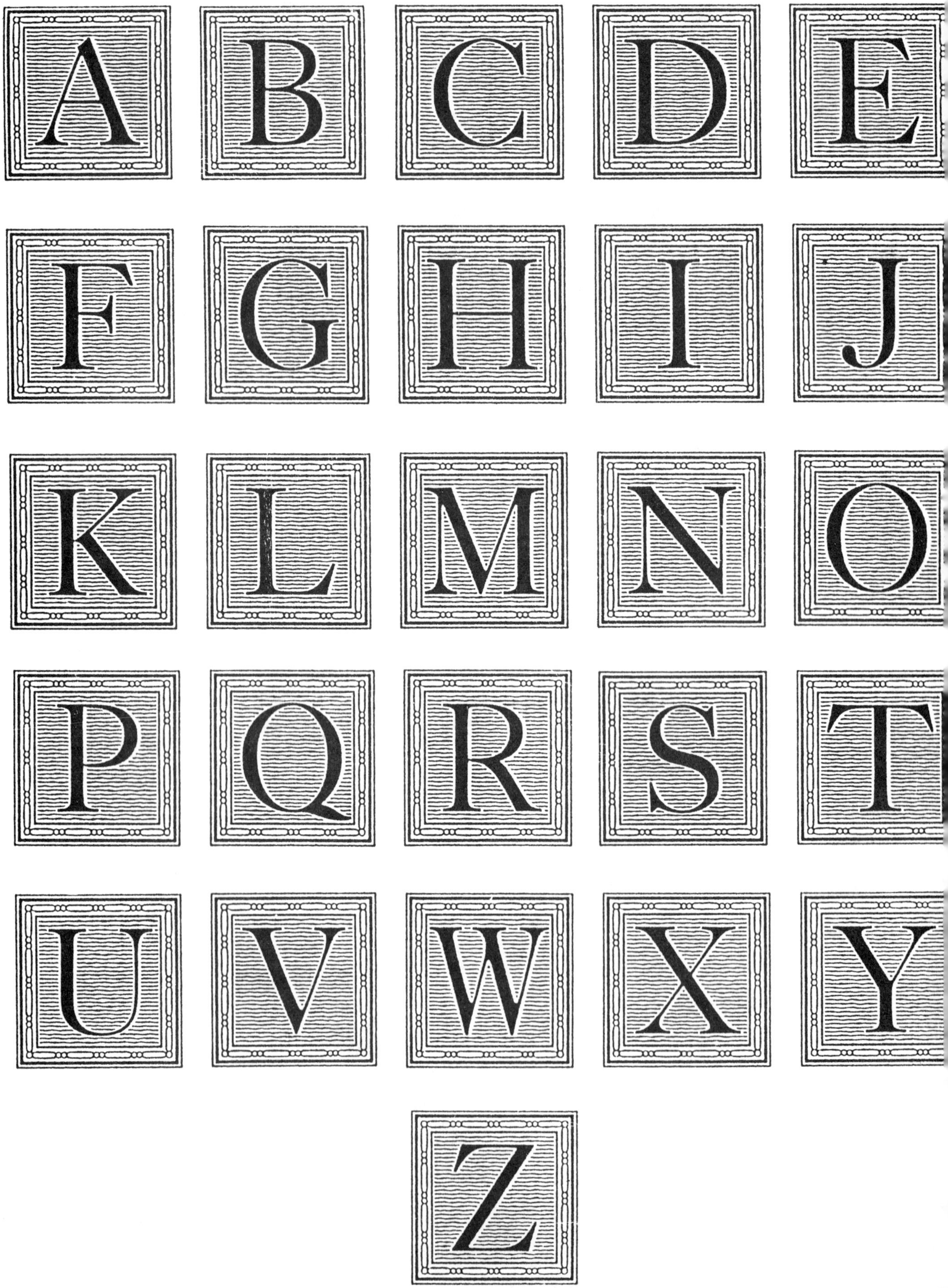

A B C D E
F G H I J
K L M N O
P Q R S T
U V W X Y
Z

Instant Graphics reproducible page, copyright © 1984

Sunday	Monday	Tuesday	Wednesday	Thursday	Friday	Saturday

0123456789

0123456789

0123456789

0123456789

0 1 2 3 4 5 6 7 8 9

0 1 2 3 4 5 6 7 8 9

0 1 2 3 4 5 6 7 8 9

0 1 2 3 4 5 6 7 8 9

January	Book Reports
February	Reading
March	Spelling
April	Writing
May	Math
June	Social Studies
July	History
August	Science
September	Art
October	Things to Do
November	**Homework**
December	Due Date
	Your Assignment

Instant Graphics reproducible page, copyright© 1984

Special Event	Bonus
Special Performance	Extra Credit
Class Play	You're Invited
Important	Happy Birthday
Help!	Happy Holidays
Remember!	Season's Greetings
Thanks	**Sign-Up List**
Congratulations!	Announcing
Have Fun!	Newsletter
Award	Class News
Special Award	Meeting
Certificate	
Certificate of Achievement	

Index

Alphabets, 112-118
Animals
  bats, 87, 104
  birds, 54, 59, 60-62, 74, 76, 81, 82, 85, 91, 96, 102
  butterflies, 54, 60, 77, 94, 95, 100
  cows, 104
  dinosaurs, 105
  dog, 90
  ducks/geese, 103, 106
  frogs, 106
  spider/spiderweb, 60
  tigers, 105
  turkey, 105
  whales, 106
Baskets, 55, 67, 82
Binding techniques, 41
Boats, 91, 92
Books, 56, 62, 63
Borders. *See also* Frames.
  circular or oval, 52, 53, 59, 65
  rectangular and square, 50, 51, 54, 55, 60, 64-68, 110
  scenic or elaborate, 69-93, 101, 107, 108
Calendar grid, 119
Candles, 58, 63
Cattails, 67
Flowers
  crocus, 73
  daisies, 62, 70, 75, 81, 89, 92, 102
  fuchsia, 79
  iris, 86, 87
  lilies, 71
  pansies, 96
  roses, 61, 67, 69, 72, 77, 78, 85, 100, 101
  snowdrops, 76, 83
  violets, 88, 98
  wildflowers, 74, 84, 95, 102
Frames. *See also* Borders.
  for headings, 52-54, 56, 57, 63
  for messages, 108
Grapes/grapevines, 66
Headings, 122, 123
Holiday art
  Christmas, 80, 109-112
  Easter (lilies), 71
  Halloween (bats), 87, 104
  Thanksgiving (turkey), 105
Holly, 80, 109, 110, 112
Houses, 83, 93
Human faces and figures, 61, 63, 88-90, 98, 102-104, 107, 108, 111

Leaves, 99, 100, 104
Mock-up, 22
Moon, 87
Mountains, 71, 95, 97
Musical instruments, 50, 63
Nature prints, 9-10
Numbers, 120, 121
Ornamental art, 58-64
Paste-up guide, 22
Postcard insignia, 110
Scenes, 69-99, 102-104
Seasonal art
  fall, 66, 68, 89, 93, 96
  spring, 54, 55, 71, 81, 82, 86-88, 98, 101, 102
  summer, 69, 70, 72-79, 84, 85, 91, 92, 95, 97, 99, 103, 104
  winter, 80, 83, 90, 94
Styrofoam tray printing, 10
Theater-related art, 52, 60
Thistle, 62
Trees, 84, 86, 88, 90, 91, 93-95, 97-99, 103, 104
Water (lakes, ocean, rivers), 71, 86, 87, 91-95, 97, 9 102-104
Wheat, 68, 89, 96, 97